THE HORSEMAN OF THE SHENANDOAH

A reproduction of the earliest portrait of George Washington by John Singleton Copley. It is now owned by Charles F. Worel of London who has given permission to reproduce it.

THE
HORSEMAN
OF THE
SHENANDOAH

A BIOGRAPHICAL ACCOUNT
OF THE EARLY DAYS OF
George Washington

By BLISS ISELY

THE BRUCE PUBLISHING COMPANY
MILWAUKEE

Library of Congress Catalog Card Number: 62–15224

© 1962 The Bruce Publishing Company
MADE IN THE UNITED STATES OF AMERICA

Contents

THE HORSEMAN OF THE SHENANDOAH

The forks of the Ohio and surrounding territory

I. *Forks of the Ohio*

IF IT had not been for the West the East never could have amounted to much. Two hundred years ago the East was a mere shoestring on the map, like Chile or Norway, hemmed in between the Atlantic breakers and the Allegheny barricade.

Before the East could unlock the West it had to gain a triangle of land now included in a 36-acre park in Pittsburgh where two rivers, the Allegheny and the Monongahela, merge into the Ohio. Whoever commanded the point between the Forks of the Ohio could prevent anyone else from navigating either fork. Whoever was master there could float flatboats down the Ohio and pre-empt a potential treasureland of wheat, cotton, wool, cattle, petroleum, coal, lead, zinc, iron, copper, silver, and gold.

A Virginian of that remote era, wishing to journey to the Forks of the Ohio, followed deer trails west from Wills Creek, now Cumberland, through the Narrows that notch the Alleghenies, thrashed through brambles of laurel and scrub, edged around sharp and precipitous rocks, and in a few miles found himself at the headsprings of a branch of the Monongahela. The difficulties would be hard to appreciate today on the smooth drive through the Narrows on U. S. Highway 40, but 200 years ago the Virginian, after passing the Narrows, still had to fight through more laurel and scrub and forest and mountain and mire to get down to the point of the triangle between the Forks.

On the other hand, a resident of the French province of

1

Canada, going to the Forks, sallied out of Montreal in bateau or canoe, singing as he unreefed the sail or plied the paddle. Up the St. Lawrence he sped, portaging the Lachine Rapids, crossing Lake Ontario, portaging Niagara Falls, hugging the south shore of Lake Erie until he came to Presque Isle, now called Erie. There he ascended a creek to the carrying place, portaged his craft a mile to a southbound stream, floated on it into the Allegheny and down the Allegheny to the Forks. It was hard voyaging, but by comparison so much easier than the route from Virginia that the French were on the Ohio long ahead of the English.

A thin handful they were, but a swaggering Frenchman would as lief bash in the head of an Englishman as skin a skunk; in fact, liefer — he had no animosity toward a skunk. Consequently no man with an English tongue, except the resourceful, the reckless, and the audacious, ventured through the Narrows to measure swagger against swagger.

Yet there were those who envisaged an English establishment beyond the mountains, among them Virginia's governor, Robert Dinwiddie, who could see rainbows in the West. According to the polite diplomacy of the time, it was necessary, before he took steps to secure the Ohio in the name of England's king, that he first dispatch a note to the French commandant there, warning that he and his countrymen should get out and smartly.

Casting for a daredevil to deliver the ultimatum, Dinwiddie found counselors who advised that none was more mighty in valor than William Trent, who had mocked the French by trading with the Indians of the West. Acting on the counsel, the governor commissioned Trent and sent as a companion, William Russell, a man of address and boldness approaching that of Trent. It was pleasant early September when these tough wayfarers came to the Forks. At that juncture each apparently asked the other: "What good is a hero without his scalp?" Question followed question until they scared each other into retreating to the east side of the mountains, where they reported that nobody could make it to the French commandant at Le Boeuf alive. If these two could not get through, then who could?

Prompt action was imperative, for the king's ministers in London had informed Dinwiddie that their spies in Quebec had discovered how the French governor in Canada had designed a fort on the Ohio around which France could muster a colony to serve as a growing rampart of men supplementing the barricade of the mountains. Dinwiddie needed somebody to warn the French to get out and stay out.

The theory has been advanced by most of George Washington's early biographers that Dinwiddie asked him to go where Trent and Russell had failed. On the contrary, circumstantial evidence indicates that Dinwiddie would never have thought of Washington in this connection.

True, it may have come to the governor's attention that Washington could outride, outleap, outrun, and outthrow anybody he had ever met. The governor may have learned that since the age of sixteen Washington had been a frontier surveyor who could build a fire in a rain, kill a deer, cook it himself, and, on occasion, could bed down in a snowdrift with reasonable comfort. But what of it? Virginia had other frontier surveyors more mature than Washington. The governor was not looking for a decathlon champion.

That Dinwiddie did not rate Washington too highly is evident from the fact that when the surveyor asked to be named major of the militia of northwest Virginia's frontier, the governor passed him over, naming him major of the region on the friendly North Carolina border, a post of least responsibility and no consequence. The idea that he could deliver a message to Le Boeuf must have originated in no place other than in Washington's own creative mind. He must have told himself: "Virginia wants to replace the French on the Ohio. Dinwiddie wants to send an ultimatum. Here's my chance to demonstrate who's the up-and-coming young man of this colony."

At any rate the 21-year-old surveyor went horseback in 1753 out of the Shenandoah Valley down the dirt road toward the Virginia capital of Williamsburg. Since Trent's fiasco, the season had advanced. Already the Big Dipper was heralding approaching snow by cowering to the horizon far below the North Star in the evening sky. Already nature, knowing that the leaves of the forest must soon die, had splashed them with ten thousand colors to give them a last fling of gaiety before they fell.

It surpasses belief that anyone would volunteer so late in the year to ride beyond those mountains which turned back the Atlantic breezes that otherwise might have tempered the snow and ice. But Washington was not to be fazed by portents of cold. His heart was attuned with the mockingbirds whose late October rhapsodies sounded the ecstasies of May.

Into Williamsburg he rode and turned into the dusty drive leading to the governor's palace. It is possible that 16-year-old Elizabeth Dinwiddie and her younger sister, Rebecca, enjoying the Indian summer sun on the upstairs balcony, saw him coming. If they did, they looked twice, for Washington, whether afoot or ahorse, was worth looking at long. Years later Thomas Jefferson was to write that Washington was the greatest horseman of his time. Here he was, galloping with the grace of a centaur.

A Negro, recognizing him as one who on previous visits had always tipped the hostler, flashed a grin and then stood attentively at the iron gate of the low brick wall that separated the drive from the palace forecourt. The horseman swung from the saddle, tossed the reins to the hostler, and in No. 11 boots strode the 25 paces up the walk leading to the palace door.

He reached for the knocker with a hand so large that the glove fitting it had to be made to order. Admitted to the reception hall, he inhaled the fragrance of autumn flowers cut that morning from the 10-acre palace gardens and arranged as directed by Mrs. Dinwiddie, hostess of the grandest residence in the 13 colonies. As he waited for the doorman to take his name to the governor, the caller had time to notice the imported marble floor, the paneled walls of Virginia walnut, and the racks of grim flintlocks on one wall and burnished sabers on the other.

Ushered into the presence of the governor, Washington bowed like a courtier, for although callused hands, muscled shoulders, and lean flanks indicated he was one who lived outdoors by the strength that was in him, he also was versed in the manners the Virginia gentry had borrowed from England. The 60-year-old governor looked up into the eyes of the surveyor, who stood six feet two above his stockings. No press secretary was present to release a news account of what passed between the two men, but we can conjecture that the governor inquired: "What brings you, Major Washington?"

And the major responded: "Sir, I'll put your ultimatum into the hands of the French commandant!"

Perhaps the governor hesitated. More likely his heart warmed to this healthy, young, self-reliant frontiersman. He must have assayed his visitor's pock-pitted face, which meant that he could go to any infected camp and be immune to smallpox.

Doubtless the two conferred for hours. The governor arranged finances so that his ambassador could hire a French interpreter and also men who could speak to the Indians of different tribes. No doubt the governor, famed for his hospitality, invited the major to dinner with the family, and no doubt Washington, who had no fear of the bluff governor but was afraid of girls, looked down into his plate as he sat with Elizabeth and Rebecca.

After dinner, Dinwiddie wrote an ultimatum to the French commandant, which read:

"The Lands upon the River Ohio in the Western Parts of this Colony of Virginia are so notoriously known to be the Property of the Crown of Great Britain, that it is a Matter of equal Concern and Surprise to me to hear that a Body of French Forces are erecting Fortresses and making Settlements upon that River within his Majesties Domain."

Signing his dispatch and affixing his signet, the governor wrapped it in an oilskin pouch, shook the big hand of the big major, and watched him ride away. How could the governor know that in eight short months this brash, ambitious, self-assured young man would set aclang the tocsin of war beyond the Narrows, a clang that would sound and resound across the Atlantic to Europe, enflaming the world to the jungles of the Ganges? How could the governor guess that before another autumn, Washington's name would be on every Virginia tongue or that his deeds would be toasted in the coffeehouses of London or cursed in the salons of Paris?

II. *An Athlete Hunts a Job*

IN CASE the bigwigs of Williamsburg questioned the wisdom of sending Washington on a wintry ride on a mission in which Trent and Russell had failed, they could have gone to Fredericksburg and Winchester and found many western men with confidence in this young fellow.

At Fredericksburg they would have learned that Washington at the age of fifteen already was recognized as a man. He already was running surveying lines. Since he was unlicensed, his maps had to be signed by an authorized person to make them official, and George had to split the fees, but he was doing the actual work and building a reputation.

His big chance was just ahead one February morning in 1748 at about the time of his sixteenth birthday when he rose in a chill upstairs room of his mother's eight-room house and dressed as he had done in that same room 3000 times before. With his brothers, Sam, Jack, and Charles, he descended to the first floor where they greeted their mother and their sister, Betty. To the breakfast table the family filed where all bowed as George, standing beside his chair, read grace from an Anglican prayer book, a task his mother had assigned to him upon his father's death five years earlier. From now on Sam, next in age, would be the man of the house and read the prayers.

Sometime after breakfast one of Mrs. Washington's slaves brought a horse to the mounting block and held the stirrup. It is probable that George packed his father's compass and

7

other surveying instruments into his saddlebags. At least he had such instruments when he reached his destination.

Then, after good-bys were said, George took the 60-mile muddy road for Mount Vernon, home of his 30-year-old half-brother, Lawrence. There was nothing remarkable about the journey. George had been there before. For six miles he skirted the winding Rappahannock River to the northwest before taking a more northerly direction to Lawrence's home on the Potomac.

At a bend of the road he probably looked back for a farewell view of his mother's square frame house. Soon Fredericksburg on the south side of the river, opposite his mother's home, also passed from sight.

The boys of the community missed him after he had gone. Then other things demanded their attention. A few years later, however, when news of what George was doing at the Forks of the Ohio came back to Virginia, his former companions took pride in relating tales of his prowess. They kept telling of his exploits through the years and continued telling them after they became old men. Perhaps they stretched the yarns, for good stories tend to improve with retelling.

So terrific was the strength of his fingers, so they said, he could balance a Spanish silver dollar on his fore and middle fingers and double it by pressure with his thumb.

Another account that has lived through two centuries has it that a group of neighborhood boys were gathered on a bank of the Rappahannock hurling pieces of slate over the water. Since the river was 300 feet wide, according to surveys of the time, it was apparently impossible to throw across it. The boys could tell who threw the farthest by noting where the slates splashed in the water.

When it came George's turn, he picked up a piece of slate — some accounts say it was a Spanish dollar — and let fly. It rose high in the air, glinting in the sunlight. Instead of splash-

ing, it spanned the river with 30 paces to spare on the far side.
A throw of 390 feet! This is about the distance from far center
field to the home plate of a baseball diamond. What a center
fielder! By comparison, the world's record baseball throw was
made by Don Grate of Chattanooga of 443 feet 3½ inches in
1953.

There was his mother's stallion, so vicious that none dared attempt to ride him. George sprang to his back. The steed reared,
pawed the air, careened, bucked. It seemed he would snap the
rider's neck, yet George rode and rode and rode until the
animal, red-eyed, foaming, blood streaming from its nostrils,
fell dead. What a broncho buster!

The debunkers deride some of the tales as unproved. And
yet their similarity of pattern is evidence of their general truth.
After he had reached the age of 50, George picked up an iron
bar and hurled it farther than any of the young athletes could
throw it.

Sloshing toward Mount Vernon, George had ample time to
reflect on the gap separating him from his half brothers. The
law of primogeniture, prevailing at that day, provided the best
of everything to the eldest. And so, Augustine Washington, the
father, sent his two elder sons to Appleby's School in England.
Lawrence studied there seven years and, among other things,
learned military drill and surveying. George would study both
under him. Augustine, Jr., known to his brothers as Austin,
attended for a shorter time, yet long enough to carry on the
family name with grace if Lawrence should not live.

When Father Washington came to die at 49, he left his
largest plantation, covering 2500 acres, to Lawrence. Austin
inherited the next largest acreage. A comparatively small part
was left to Augustine's second wife, Mary Ball Washington, in
trust for her children. Each was to have a portion at the age
of 21 and the remainder upon her death. George's share was

larger than that of his younger brothers and sister, but even so it amounted to only 280 acres, large enough for a middle class farmer, but so inadequate for Washington's ambition that he did not claim it when he became 21. Instead, he left it with his mother, taking possession only after her death, which occurred when he was 57 and President of the United States.

Lawrence not only was head of the House of Washington, and rich; he was distinguished. Shortly after his return from school in England, he volunteered to fight Spain in the War of Jenkins Ear, so named from the fact that it was precipitated when a Spanish officer allegedly slashed off with a sword the ear of a British merchant captain named Jenkins. Governor Gooch, who commanded the Virginians in the war, named Lawrence captain of one of the four Virginia companies.

The Virginians sailed in the fleet of Admiral Edward Vernon, in whose honor Lawrence later named his estate Mount Vernon. He served creditably in the West Indies, on the Isthmus of Panama, and in the befuddled Cartagena campaign, in which Vernon directed the troops to flounder through the swamps to attack the walled city of Cartagena from the rear. They were supplied with ladders too short to scale the walls, but did not know it until they reached the city, where the mocking Spaniards shot at them. Forced to retreat, they regained the ships, their faces blotched from bites of malarial mosquitoes. Lawrence came home, shaking with ague and emaciated. Later he developed a persistent cough, which he attributed to the hardships of the campaign.

Governor Gooch honored him by appointing him as adjutant of all the Virginia militia with the rank of major. His district elected him to the House of Burgesses. When Virginians discussed big things, Lawrence was called on to help make decisions. He married Anne Fairfax, daughter of a near neighbor, Colonel William Fairfax, master of Belvoir and cousin of Lord

Thomas Fairfax, who had title to 5,000,000 acres of Virginia land.

George was proud of his brother. He, too, wanted to be a major of militia, a Burgess, and the owner of 2500 acres of land. But the only way he could think of getting it was to become a licensed surveyor. Pay for surveying was good, employment fairly steady. With his earnings he might marry near nobility and own a plantation.

At Mount Vernon he practiced surveying under Lawrence's eye. The plat of one of these surveys, that of a turnip patch, is still extant. The plat is well drawn and the wording is well lettered. The half-literate tutors, who had instructed him to spell badly and to punctuate worse, grounded him well in drawing and mathematics and gave him a smattering of surveying.

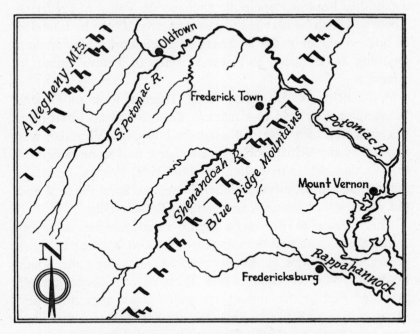

Where Washington was employed as a surveyor

One day, taking a vacation from his practice, George rode to Belvoir to call on George William Fairfax, 22-year-old brother-in-law of Lawrence. There he met Lord Thomas Fairfax, who was living temporarily with his cousin.

His lordship had fallen in love with Virginia's trees, mountains, tide flats, rains, sunshine, and fox hunting, and decided to spend the rest of his years in America, developing his 5,000,000 acre estate. It extended between the Potomac and Rappahannock rivers westward across the Blue Ridge and the Shenandoah and South Potomac valleys to the roof of the Allegheny Mountains.

Already squatters were settling west of the Blue Ridge. Fairfax needed to have the land surveyed so that he could assign farms to the squatters and collect rent. He already had established headquarters in the Shenandoah Valley at Frederick Town to which he planned to move shortly. There he intended to build a manor house and oversee a seigniory greater than anything in England and second only to Penn's estate in America.

A bachelor of 55 years, Lord Thomas took to George Washington like steel to a magnet. George was no smart-alec, wise-cracking teen-ager. Although he knew any Virginian was as good as any British noble, he also knew how to be respectful to his elders. More than that, he could ride. Fairfax, an adept man in the saddle, admired other horsemen. Soon the lord and the youth were chasing foxes over the Belvoir Hills.

There came to Belvoir a highly rated frontier surveyor, James Genn, who had been engaged by Lord Thomas to make preliminary surveys in the Shenandoah and along the South Potomac. Whether Genn, Lord Thomas, or George himself proposed that he accompany the party as an apprentice surveyor, the records are lacking. We do know, that a few days later on March 12, 1748, George was at the crest of Ashby's

Gap through which U. S. Highway 50 today passes the Blue Ridge. Forest trees hampered the view below so that George could not look down past his stirrups into the Valley of the Daughter of the Stars — Shenandoah.

There was, however, enough of a break in the branches so that, not quite lost in the haze of distance, he could see the Alleghenies, beyond which water flowed westward into the Ohio. Possibly George conjured up a picture of himself doing things out there that would win for him fame as great as that of James Genn or Tom Cresap. If he did, he kept it secret even from his diary. Three days later, however, he found something worth confiding in his diary, when, after a night in the home of Captain Isaac Pennington in the Shenandoah, he wrote: "we got our Supper & was Lighted into a Room & I not being so good a Woodsman as ye rest of my Company striped myself very orderly & went into ye Bed as they call it when to my Surprise I found it to be nothing but a Little Straw-Matted together without Sheets or anything else but only one thread Bear blanket with double its weight of Vermin such as Lice, Fleas &c I was glad to get up (as soon as ye Light was carried from us) I put on my Cloths & Lay as my Companions. Had we not been very tired I am sure we should not have Slep'd much that night."

The next evening he added: "We set out early & finished about one o'Clock & then Travell'd up to Frederick Town where our Baggage came to us we cleaned ourselves (to get Rid of y. Game we had catched y. Night before.)"*

---

* Quotations of George Washington in this and succeeding chapters are from his original writings as copied exactly or edited by the following:

John C. Fitzpatrick, ed., *The Diaries of George Washington, 1748–1799*, Vol. I (Boston-New York: Houghton-Mifflin Co.), published for the Mount Vernon Ladies Association of the Union, 1925.

John C. Fitzpatrick, ed., *The Writings of George Washington from the Original Manuscripts, 1745–1799* (Washington: U. S. Printing Office, 1931).

John C. Fitzpatrick, ed., *George Washington, Colonial Traveler, 1732–1775* (Indianapolis: Bobbs Merrill Co., 1927).

From Frederick Town the surveyors moved north to the Potomac River to survey tracts occupied by squatters. Raw March winds brought pelting rains. Genn, tired of continual drenching, took his men across the Potomac in canoes as they swam their horses. They were now in Maryland, not far from the frontier home of Tom Cresap, who lived at the abandoned Shawnee village of Oldtown, a dozen miles southeast of the present Cumberland.

Since this fabulous pioneer was famed for his hospitality, Genn sought shelter there. For three days the men lounged before the fireplace and feasted on venison, smoked ham, wild ducks, and other food from the Cresap larder. We have reason to believe that in those three days, while rain swished the window panes and swashed the shakes of the roof, George sat spellbound, listening to word pictures of Cresap's vivid experiences. We can believe this because Cresap was a capital storyteller. He continued relating his tales to anyone who would listen until he died at the age of 106. It would be contrary to his nature if he remained silent as he looked at George.

"Young fellow," he might have remarked, "I was fifteen, not quite as old as you and not near as big when I came to America. I was a green Yorkshire lad."

Jared Sparks, ed., *The Writings of George Washington,* Vol. II, Boston, 1834.

Washington's manuscript written for David Humphries, first published by *Scribner's Magazine,* May, 1893.

III. *The Fabulous Cresap*

CERTAINLY in those three days Cresap must have described the teeming beaver colonies that dammed the creeks and rivers in the region centering at the Forks of the Ohio. He must have told how the French from Canada and the English from Pennsylvania were pugnaciously competing for the trade of the Indians of that area, how the Indians had no knowledge of the fabulous prices paid for beaver skins on the Paris and London markets, and how a healthy young fellow who did not mind risking a poniard in his back could grow rich in the beaver trade.

He probably told how Thomas Joncaire was stolen from his home in Canada by a Seneca Indian, how he came to love the Indian way of life and married a Seneca woman, and how he built his home on the Allegheny River and became the chief of the French traders there. Joncaire was ruthless with Pennsylvanians who came into the domain he had pre-empted, until he died in 1740 bequeathing his business and the good will of the Indians to his swarthy and crafty sons, Philippe and Daniel.

His sons were as ruthless as the father, but a year after the death of Thomas there arrived John Frazier, a new kind of competitor from Pennsylvania. He settled at the Delaware Indian village of Venango on the site of the present Franklin, Pennsylvania, where he traded for furs just like the Joncaires. But he added a blacksmith shop, transporting by packhorses an anvil and tools from across the mountains. This attracted

15

Delawares, Shawnees, Wyandottes, and other Indians to his trading post to have their broken knives repaired, their leaking kettles made whole, and their gunlocks mended. Since none of the Frenchmen had skill in such things, Frazier became indispensable to the Indians. The Joncaires would have knifed him in a minute, but to do so would alienate the tribesmen, and Frazier chuckled derisively at his enemies.

Just three years after Frazier opened his shop, the kings of France and England went blithely to war over who should sit on the throne of Austria. Their armies fought in what Englishmen call the War of Austrian Succession, but which in America is more commonly called King George's War. The English navy blockaded the French ports or ran down French merchantmen on the seas so that very few French ships could cross the Atlantic to bring goods to the Canadian traders. The Joncaires were practically out of business, and that made it good for the Pennsylvanians.

They swarmed into the Ohio country to trade for furs. As many as 400 came in a single season, transporting manufactured articles by packhorse to the Indian villages and returning with fortunes in beaver skins. Prince of them all was George Croghan, who centered his operations at the Delaware village of Logstown, about 18 miles down the Ohio from the present Pittsburgh.

With his half brother, Edward Ward, and his brother-in-law, William Trent, he voyaged down the Ohio to the Wyandotte settlement at the mouth of the Muskingum to trade new kettles, knives, vermilion, looking glasses, beads, and other manufactured goods dear to the Indians for furs. With a few companions he even journeyed as far as Lake Michigan, where he induced a large number of the Miamis to migrate to the Miami River in the present Ohio and build the village of Pickawillany where the city of Piqua now stands. Their chief, called Demoisselle by the French, became so fond of the English that they re-named him Old Briton. Some Ottawas from Detroit and Illinois from the Mississippi country came with their skins to trade at Logstown for English goods.

Cresap had nothing against particular Pennsylvanians, such as Croghan or Frazier, but he hated Pennsylvania in general. He had once settled in a no-man's region between Pennsylvania and Maryland, which both colonies claimed. Pennsylvania officers arrested him for trespass and confined him in a Philadelphia jail for a year. It hurt him to see all that wealth flowing to that city.

And so he discussed the Ohio fur trade with rich and influential Virginians with the upshot that ten of them joined with Cresap to form the Ohio Company of Virginia. They added to the partnership John Hanbury, a London merchant, who could sell their beaver packs on the London market and also gain access to the king through the British Lords of Trade. Washington knew about the Ohio Company, for both of his half brothers, Lawrence and Austin, were partners, as was George William Fairfax, Lawrence's brother-in-law.

They petitioned the king to exclude Pennsylvania from the Ohio and to grant the company exclusive rights there together with 200,000 acres of land on the south bank of the Ohio between the Forks of that river and the Great Kanawha. On their part they offered to build a fort on the Ohio and garrison it at their own expense. They also agreed to settle at least 100 families on the land within seven years. In case they settled the 100 families, they asked that the king grant them 300,000 acres more.

Governor William Gooch, sometimes rated as the best governor colonial Virginia ever had, liked the plan so well that he joined the company as a thirteenth partner. He was a patriot first, but he saw no sin in making a doubloon out of patriotism. He forwarded the plan with his approval to the king.

King George II had but to dip quill in ink and sign his name and the Ohio would be added to his realm with no cost to the crown. But the king dillydallied.

All through 1747 he did nothing. Then came 1748. The French and English ministers began talking of peace. The alarmed Virginians had hoped to be established on the Ohio with 100 families and a stout fort before the making of peace. They knew that once peace was consummated, French cargoes again would cross the Atlantic, French traders would paddle down from Montreal with trade goods, and the task of winning the trade with the Indians would be more difficult.

But the king continued to dillydally, and because he did, the blood of many a British boy would soak the mast on the forest floor at the forks of the Ohio, and many a blond scalp would dangle in the smoke of western wigwams.

Between Cresap's tales of the West, Washington had opportunity to observe his herds of cattle and hogs and to enjoy the frontier comforts of his well-built house. He had opportunity to learn that the pioneer and his wife Hannah always kept a latchstring out for Indians as well as for white people.

When Indians came in large parties, Cresap killed a hog for them and cooked it in a great outdoor iron kettle, mixing the chunks of pork with corn, beans, and greens. He hung a half-quart ladle beside the kettle so that any Indian could dip into it and eat his fill. From the ladle he was known to the Indians as "Big Spoon." From his western position and from his friendly communication with the Indians, he was invaluable to the Ohio Company. He always had the latest news from the West.

It is to be regretted that George did not write in his diary the things that Cresap told him. His only entry for the three days reads: "Rain'd till about two oClock and Clear'd when we were agreeably Surpris'd at y. sight of Thirty odd Indians Coming from War with only one Scalp we had some Liquor with us of which we gave them Part it elevated their spirits and put them in y. Humor of Dauncing of whom we had a War Daunce There manner of Dauncing is as follows Viz they clear a Large Circle and make a Great Fire in y. middle then Seats Themselves around it y. Speaker makes a grand Speech telling them in what Manner They are to Daunce after he has finished y. best Dauncer jumps up as one awakened out of a Sleep and runs and jumps about y. Ring in a most Comical Manner he is followed by y. Rest then Begins there Musicians to Play ye Musick is a Pot half of Water with a deerskin stretched over it as tight as it can and a goard with some Shott in it to Rattle and a piece of a horses Tail tied to it to make it look fine y. one Keeps Rattling and y. other Drumming and all y. while y. others Dauncing."

IV. *Life in the Gristle*

LEAVING the comforts of Cresap's dwelling, Genn led his surveyors across the Potomac into the Fairfax domain, southwestward into a wilderness where only here and there could be found the cabin of a gristly squatter in the valley of the South Branch of the Potomac. The Shenandoah seemed civilized by comparison. Here, occasionally the party came upon Indian hunters.

A laconic entry in Washington's diary reads: "With Indians all day." He was learning at firsthand the character of the red men, with whom he would have to deal at the council fire in the years just ahead. He was learning to palaver with them and to win their respect because of his athletic ability.

Genn had provided packhorses to carry provisions, but mostly they lived on wild meat. The South Branch was a veritable larder with deer, elk, and turkeys to be had for the shooting. Each surveyor took turns at providing meat. At that time Washington was only an amateur hunter. Now he was turning professional. He had to kill or go hungry. After his first assignment as hunter, he entered ruefully in his diary: "Shot twice at wild turkeys but missed." But he improved. Another entry reads: "Shot two wild turkeys." In time he would become a backwoods sharpshooter and could live by his gun.

He also became adept at outdoor cookery, as is shown by this report: "After we had pitched our Tent and made a very Large Fire we pulled out our knapsack in order to Recruit ourselves every [one] was his own Cook our Spits was Forked Sticks our Plates a Large Chip as for Dishes we had none."

Once they stopped at a cabin where Washington was disappointed at not finding the conveniences of home, for he wrote: "When we came to supper there was neither cloth upon ye. Table nor a knife to eat with as good luck would have it we had knives of our own."

Although the backwoodsmen were unlettered, Washington learned to regard his new associates for what they were rather than to disparage them for what they were not. They taught him how to tell directions in the woods on a cloudy day by noting the moss on the trees or the direction in which the top branches inclined before the prevailing winds. What was more important, he learned more about surveying than he ever could have picked up in college.

After little more than a year as an apprentice, Washington journeyed to Williamsburg to stand for an examination at William and Mary College. Without benefit of classroom instruction, he passed the tests and was awarded a certificate as a fully qualified surveyor. He agreed, as the certificate was issued, to contribute to the college one sixth of his fees as a surveyor for as long as he practiced. A few weeks later, at the age of 17, he was appointed surveyor of Culpepper County. Lord Fairfax had large holdings there and had confidence in Washington's ability to survey them. On July 20, 1749, he officially took his first public office and on that date filed his commission at the Culpepper County courthouse. This appointment gave sanction to surveys George might make not only in the County but anywhere else in Virginia.

For the next few years he was the chief surveyor of Lord Fairfax, working for the most part in the Shenandoah Valley. While the Fairfax manor house was not built, his lordship made his residence at Frederick Town. There Washington often stopped for consultation. He made his headquarters in a cabin of hewn logs nearby, where, after completing field work, he could find shelter for his map making and other office work. The cabin still stands in Winchester, the name Lord Fairfax later gave to Frederick Town.

On field trips, Washington spread his blankets on the ground and in midsummer woke as the early light kindled the loftier summits of the forest-hooded mountains to the West. If it rained, he raised a tent if he had one. Otherwise he hastily arranged a half-faced hut of bark and slept there like an Indian. If he came near a settler's cabin, the frontiersmen, who were invariably hospitable and glad to entertain a stranger who had news, invited him to eat and enjoy the available shelter. In a letter to a friend, Washington wrote: "I have not sleep'd above three nights or four in a bed but after walking all Day lay down before the fire upon a Little Hay Straw Fodder or bairskin whichever it is to be had with Man wife and children like a parcel of Dogs or Catts & happy he that gets the Berth nearest the fire there's nothing would make it pass tolerably but a good Reward a Dubbleloon is my constant gain every Day that the Weather will permit my going and sometimes six pistoles . . . I have never had my cloths of but lay like a Negro except a few Nights I have lay'n in Frederick Town."

Imagine a 17-year-old boy earning a doubloon a day! A doubloon was a Spanish gold coin valued at $14 in the present worth of United States gold. A pistole was a Spanish silver coin valued at about $3.50. And the buying power was much greater than money of the same weight today.

It gave Washington money to invest in land. As a surveyor he had ample opportunity to study and to know land. Frequent entries in his diary show how well he understood the difference between fertility and the lack of it. By the time he was twenty he owned 2008 acres, all earned at surveying.

The longer he surveyed, the greater did Washington's reputation grow as a man who knew the frontier. The plantation owners took note of him, but it was among the illiterates of the border that he became a legend. Their world was very small. Without newspapers or books and without the ability to read them if they had them, they talked mostly of each other.

Around the winter fires they told of the surveyor who could measure land, figure out the number of acres in a given area, and could put it all down on a map. And they told of his physical prowess. On one occasion, so the tale runs, he approached a frontier cabin to find a group of young men jumping. Among the interested spectators was a 16-year-old girl, belle of the frontier, where men were so numerous that every lass had her selection of suitors. This girl was so popular that her father, to prevent violence if she selected one and rejected the others, arranged the jumping match. He who jumped the farthest could marry the girl.

Washington, arriving as they were jumping and, knowing nothing of the prize, took a running start. We must believe that the girl uttered a prayer in her heart. Tall, slender, and clean he was. What a husband! Earning a doubloon or six pistoles a day, what a provider!

At the mark Washington took off, rose high in the air, threw his feet forward, and landed far beyond the best mark made. The father proclaimed him the winner of the delighted girl. The surveyor stammered. Apologizing, he backed away. He was afraid of girls.

V. *France Learns of the Ohio Company*

WHILE Washington was making money and toughening himself for his career, his brothers, Lawrence and Austin, and their associates of the Ohio Company were fretting. Every ship that came up the Potomac, they watched eagerly for word that the King had approved their colony on the Ohio. Surely the next vessel or the next after would bring the long-wanted message.

In 1748 King George agreed to a treaty with King Louis of France, ending the war. It was still not too late. The Virginians still could cross the mountains before the French could come in force. John Hanbury, the London partner, called frequently at the ministry to stand, hat in hand, and urge that somebody dip quill in ink and put it in the king's hand.

A French ambassador came from Paris to the king's court at London. He drank coffee with gossipy Londoners and learned that Hanbury was promoting a scheme to establish a colony in some remote region called the Ohio. Why the Virginians wanted to go wandering into a forested wilderness, the smart London men didn't know. The ambassador smiled in evident agreement.

Languidly he rose and left the coffeehouse. But once outside, he did no dillydallying. Hastily he dispatched a message to Paris, and there, King Louis did not dillydally either.

Across the Atlantic sails carried a letter to Marquis de la Galisonniere, governor of Canada. The governor called before him 56-year-old Celoron de Blainville, a native of Canada, a fur trader, a fighter. Celoron had commanded in New England and New York in the war just closed. Previous to that he had traded with the Indians as he commanded the French posts of Fort Niagara, Detroit, and Mackinac. He knew the Ohio, too, for once he had led a war party to fight the Natchez and Chickasaws who were threatening New Orleans. He had traveled to the south by way of the Ohio.

Under him were three mighty subordinates: Pierre Contrecoeur, who later would measure wits with Washington; Philippe Joncaire, who would meet Washington on various occasions; and Coulon de Jumonville, who would die at Washington's feet.

Celoron sent Joncaire ahead to notify the Indians he was on his way to the Ohio, that he was coming to save them from the English, and that he was their ever faithful friend. In bateaux Celoron led his expedition up the Lachine Rapids and across Lake Ontario from end to end, to portage Niagara Falls and enter Lake Erie. He was on the southern shore of Lake Erie, changing to canoes, when King George signed his name to the two-year-old petition of the Ohio Company.

Celoron portaged to Lake Chautauqua, which, although it is near Lake Erie, empties into a southward-flowing stream that carried the Frenchmen to the Allegheny River. Down its current they rode to Venango. Frazier was absent from his blacksmith shop and trading post, but Celoron captured two of Frazier's men. After a stern lecture, in which he set forth that La Salle had explored the Ohio as early as 1669 and claimed the land for France, he let them go.

Although Joncaire was a master diplomat, he did not convince the Indians that the coming of Celoron was in their interest. Before the main party of the Frenchmen arrived at Logstown, the Delawares sent several chiefs to protest the trespass. The Ohio, so they declared, belonged neither to the

English nor to the French, but to the Indians. Celoron explained that the French had always been brothers to the Indians. It was the English that had crowded the Delawares out of Pennsylvania. Now they were planning to settle 100 families on the Ohio, and 100 families would be but a beginning.

His argument was of no avail. In the end Celoron told them that nothing could dissuade him. The Delawares could not back up their protest. They looked on as the party arrived in 23 long canoes with 20 French regulars, 180 Canadian militiamen, 30 Iroquois, and 23 Abenakis, every man armed.

As the flotilla neared Logstown, Croghan faded into the woods. Celoron found other traders there and threatened them with imprisonment if they did not depart and remain away. At their various villages, the Mingoes, Delawares, Shawnees, and Wyandottes were sullen and silent. At the forks of various rivers, Celoron held a ceremony in which he buried a lead plate bearing the words that the land was in the domain of King Louis. Down the Ohio the expedition floated to the mouth of the Miami. There, turning their canoe prows northward, they ascended that stream to Pickawillany, where they met Old Briton, chief of the Miamis.

The French commander told Old Briton that the Miamis and French had always been brothers to each other. To this Old Briton flung back that he was for the English. He had traded with both the French and the English and Croghan, his brother, the Buck, gave greater value. He wanted nothing to do with Celoron or his Frenchmen. From Pickawillany the flotilla moved north as far as the Miami River would float a canoe, and then the French portaged to a northbound stream, down which they floated to Lake Erie and home to Canada.

The expedition brought only an interlude to the activities of the English. As soon as Celoron was gone, Croghan came out of the woods to trade where he had left off. Frazier re-opened his blacksmith shop. That fall Daniel Lienard de Beaujeu, commandant at Detroit, who later would face Washington in mortal combat, wrote to Governor Galisonniere that 300 British traders were operating on the Ohio. It would take more than the burying of lead plates to fence out the English.

Croghan saw war. He wrote to Governor Hamilton of Pennsylvania, urging the building of a fort on the Ohio. Hamilton wanted to go ahead with the proposal, but the legislature, dominated as it was by the Friends, refused the money. Thereupon, Croghan turned to Virginia.

Celoron was back in Canada and winter was on the way before the tardy word came to Virginia from London that the petition of the Ohio Company had the approval of the king. The partners spent several months studying the qualifications of various men who might be willing to undergo the rigors of pioneering and yet lead men. They settled on 44-year-old Christopher Gist, an educated surveyor, who had founded a settlement on the Yadkin River, just across the Virginia line in North Carolina.

Gist, when offered the job, was planting corn and would not leave his farm until he had tended his crop and harvested it and until he had his smokehouse filled. The partners, convinced that Gist was the best man available, accepted his conditions. In November, 1750, Gist began mapping the Ohio. For three successive winters he followed the wilderness trails, exploring the area on both sides of the Ohio in Pennsylvania, Ohio, Kentucky, and West Virginia. At times he returned to the Yadkin, and the tales he told there fired the imagination of one of the Boone boys, Daniel, who later would be the foremost pioneer in Kentucky.

Gist built a storehouse for the Ohio Company at Wills Creek, now Cumberland, and moved his family there. He built a second storehouse on the Monongahela at the mouth of Redstone Creek. He established a settlement near the present Mount Braddock, Pennsylvania, where he built a stockade fort and brought eleven families in the spring of 1753. This was a few miles from the Youghiogheny River, a tributary of the Monongahela. He did not lead them to the Forks of the Ohio because their numbers were too few to withstand the French traders now operating on the Ohio with trade goods secured from France. Gist needed more families first.

Not only were the French hostile, but the Indians objected to families on the Ohio. Not only did the Indians object, but Pennsylvania traders claimed the territory and, with the exception of Croghan and his followers, were bitterly resentful of the Ohio Company, which, when it was strong enough, would assert its right, granted by the king, to exclusive trade. Croghan was smart enough to see that the French would oust the Pennsylvanians unless the Virginians protected them by force. He felt that the Virginians would appreciate his co-operation and provide a place for him in the West.

Meanwhile the Ohio Company suffered a blow when their most able partner, Thomas Lee, died. This was followed by the serious illness of Lawrence Washington. His cough grew worse. His doctor prescribed that he visit Virginia's mineral springs, which the Indians thought had curative value. Accompanied by George, who gave up surveying to care for his brother, he spent some months at the springs, but the water failed to heal. Next he went to London to consult learned physicians. They recommended that he go to Barbados, a tropical isle in the British West Indies off the coast of Venezuela.

He was too feeble to sail alone, so George went with him. It was a memorable voyage for George, the longest of his life. In the Barbados he associated with British gentlemen and ladies and observed men and women of high society. Accompanied by Lawrence he inspected the fort that guarded the harbor of Barbados. For the first time he saw men mount guard and drill in perfect precision. Lawrence talked at times about his service under Admiral Vernon, and George picked up ideas regarding military maneuvers.

On one occasion Lawrence and George were invited to dine at one of the best houses on Barbados. The newfangled notion that smallpox is a communicable disease and can be spread from a patient to a well person had no acceptance in Barbados. George and Lawrence sat at table with the family, including two daughters ill with smallpox. It made no difference to Lawrence. He already had had smallpox and was immune, but George came down with the disease, and for a time Lawrence had to nurse him.

The Barbados climate did Lawrence no good. After three months he sailed for the Bermudas. He thought if the climate there agreed with him, he would have Anne come from Virginia to be with him. He, therefore, sent George home to help Anne pack up. He also directed George to call on the new governor of Virginia.

Governor Gooch had retired and returned to England. The new governor was Lord Albemarle. His lordship remained in London, drawing the salary and bearing the title of governor, while Robert Dinwiddie was named lieutenant governor and was expected to do the work. Actually the Virginia people called Dinwiddie governor, and he performed the duties of that office, including the signing of bills. Dinwiddie had previously served at various posts in the colonies and had been in Virginia before. He brought his wife and two daughters, together with enough furniture for the governor's mansion. While the colony provided the house, it was the governor's duty to provide the furniture. Gooch relinquished his partner-ship in the Ohio Company to Dinwiddie, who, thereby, gained an immediate interest in the West.

George disembarked at Yorktown, obtained a horse, and rode to Williamsburg. There he saw again William and Mary College where he had passed his examination as a surveyor. He saw the sights of the colonial capital and for the first time called on the governor, who was to give him his first big chance to prove his merit. In his diary he wrote concerning Dinwiddie: "I waited upon and wa received Graciously he enquired kindly after the health of my Br. and invited me to stay and dine."

Not a word did George put in his diary about the Dinwiddie girls. He always had been shy in the presence of girls. Now, disfigured with fresh smallpox pits, he was doubly shy. From Williamsburg George went to Mount Vernon where he de-livered his message, but Anne did not go to the Bermudas. A letter from Lawrence said that the Bermuda climate had failed to help. He was convinced that he was doomed and decided that he wanted to die in Virginia.

In July, 1752, he died at Mount Vernon. His father's will provided that if Lawrence should die without children, the estate should go to George. But this will was invalidated by the fact that Lawrence left a daughter, Sarah. Three older children had died, and Sarah was a puny child, only five months old, but the fact that she survived made Lawrence's will effec-tive in place of that of his father. It provided that in case of Sarah's death, Anne should retain a life interest in Mount Vernon and that George should succeed to the property upon her death.

After the burial of Lawrence, George returned to surveying. He was busy, but had time to fall in love at least twice. Yet he was so bashful that he could not get up nerve to tell either girl. One girl he identified in a letter to a friend as his "lowland beauty." Some say this girl was Lucy Grymes, but she never had a chance to accept him, for he went no farther than to compose bad verse in her honor.

Next he fell in love with Betsy Fauntleroy. He did not tell the girl, but wrote a letter to her father, asking her hand in marriage. But Betsy and her father saw in the tall, young horseman nothing more than a frontier surveyor, who was accustomed to sleep in a half-faced camp or on a floor of a cabin with the family and dogs. She could not know that her name would be remembered only because she could have been Mrs. George Washington.

VI. *Tomahawk Justice*

WHILE George was running surveying lines in the summer of 1752, evil tidings were brought to him in the Shenandoah. For the first time he heard of Charles Langlade, whom he was to meet face to face at a later date. Langlade lived far beyond the Alleghenies, beyond the Ohio forests, beyond Lake Michigan, in a region so remote that hardly had an Englishman even heard of it.

Intrepid, restless, vivacious, Charles Langlade stirred the hearts of Ojibwas and Ottawas on a summer night when he addressed them in council in their village, which stood between the brink of Green Bay and the encircling pines. By a warm-hearted tolerance, the red men rated Langlade as one of them, for his mother was an Ottawa. By a like benevolence, a gracious white woman of Mackinac became his wife, for his father was a Frenchman.

Langlade recited to the Ottawas how their fathers had been driven from their prosperous homelands on the Ottawa River and had been vagabonds until received by the Ojibwas into their village. And who drove them from Canada? The Iroquois. And were not the Ottawas as brave as the Iroquois? They were, but the Iroquois had guns from the Dutch and later from the English.

Yes, indeed, from the hated English. Now, Old Briton was siding with the English. Langlade knew from his own ears and eyes. He had been with Celoron at Pickawillany and had heard Old Briton defy the French. Now the English had a fort

32

in Old Briton's village. It was filled with goods of every description. The Ottawas and the Ojibwas could have those goods for the taking. Langlade's eyes flashed the flame of the council fire. "Who is brave enough to follow?" he cried. "I will lead you."

He struck his tomahawk into a tree. Man after man struck the tree and joined in the war dance. At daybreak 240 warriors, mostly Ottawas and a few Ojibwas, manned their canoes. Eastward they paddled on Green Bay, cutting with the wake of their flotilla the waters that reflected the verdure of the pines. Out on the bouyant Lake Michigan they steered. Day after day they paddled through the Straits of Mackinac and down the shores of Lake Huron until they came to Detroit. There they obtained guns and powder, trailed through the forest, and came at evening to Pickawillany.

Through the night they slept, for no smart Indian fights at night. A man might die, and when he dies at night, he enters the land of the hereafter by the night gate and nevermore sees the sun. If a warrior must die, let him die by day.

Langlade awoke at the first graying of the dawn. The gray brightened to yellow, orange, and red. Then Langlade put hand to mouth and quavered the warhoop. From every vantage point echoed answering whoops. The startled Miamis, waking from the sleep of those who feed well, struggled to open their eyes, fumbled for their weapons, and darted into the warm June dawn, naked and brave, to be shot down like rabbits scurrying from their warrens.

Mothers picked up their small babies and fled, calling to the older children to come. The men formed a rear guard as they followed their families in retreat. Past the English fort they sped as the eight traders there blazed with their muskets through loopholes at the Ottawas.

Old Briton was at the point of greatest danger. Wounded,

Route of Chas. Langlade from Green Bay to Pickawillany

and like a wounded deer at bay, he fought with hopelessness for himself, but with determination to make the enemy pay. Thirty Miamis lay still beside Old Briton as the Ottawas reaped a harvest of scalps.

Now Langlade turned to the fort. Its eight English defenders could have withstood a siege for weeks. But Langlade had a plan. He fired the wigwams. Wafted on air inflated by heat, embers floated to the dry timbers of the fort to kindle a hundred fires. Fearing that the fires would reach the powder magazine, the traders dashed out. One was killed. Two escaped. Five were made prisoner.

The Ottawas quenched the fire. From the ashes they obtained more stores than they could carry. Of fighting equipment they found guns, powder, lead, flints, and tomahawks; of clothing materials, deep blue strouds, lively red strouds, blanketing, match coating, linens, calicoes, thread, needles, gartering, and women's stockings; of adornment, ribbons, vermilion, brass wire, combs, rings, looking glasses, silver jewelry, and wampum; of hardware, knives, awls, kettles of brass or tin, beaver and bear traps, hose, axes, and files; of musical instruments, jews harps, bells, and whistles.

They returned to Green Bay by way of Detroit, turning the English prisoners over to the commandant there. At Green Bay the Ottawas reveled in riches they had brought home as the reward of victory. The prisoners were sent to Quebec and from Quebec to Paris. King Louis disclaimed responsibility for the acts of the Indians, discreetly overlooking the fact that Langlade was by French standards a white man. The king returned the prisoners to England, and they eventually reached Pennsylvania.

The goods lost at Pickawillany were valued at $5,000 in present gold, but they were worth many times more by the price level of that time. What was worse, they had not been paid for. The economy of the Indian trade was based on debt. The English merchants supplied manufactured goods to the seaboard merchants of America on credit. The merchants supplied the traders on credit. The traders sold to the Indians on credit, who, after the trapping season, paid in furs. If an Indian died, his relatives frequently paid the debt. They had no compunctions against stealing or taking goods in war, but it seems never to have occurred to them they could default payment of a debt contracted.

About one third of the loot taken from the fort at Pickawillany belonged to Croghan. It put him in serious financial difficulty with the merchants in Pennsylvania, but profits from other transactions and accumulated property saved him from imprisonment.

Fall and winter came. January ushered in a new year. In April, 1753, Chevalier Pierre Paul Marin landed at what is now Erie, Pennsylvania, and there built Fort Presque Isle of chestnut logs. Fifteen miles south at the site of Weatherford, where Le Boeuf Creek joins French Creek, he built Fort Le Boeuf, so named for the abundance of wood buffalo, a humpless species of bison that provided beef.

He directed Philippe Joncaire, now commissioned a captain, to descend French Creek to where it debouches into the Allegheny River. There, at Venango, he seized two employees of Frazier and sent them as prisoners to Montreal. Frazier again was absent and thus escaped capture. A daring man, Frazier bought more goods and built a new fort where Turtle Creek joins the Monongahela in what is now the eastern Pittsburgh suburbs. The Indians of the Ohio counted 2300 French soldiers, Canadian militiamen, half breeds, and French Indians at Presque Isle, Le Boeuf, and Venango. Over Frazier's blacksmith shop they saw floating the lilies of France.

The Delawares, Mingoes, Miamis, and Wyandottes conferred

with the English at Fairfax' home in Frederick Town, now called Winchester. They debated with Virginians representing Dinwiddie. The same delegation visited representatives of Governor Hamilton at Carlisle. All the Indians got were promises.

English prestige ebbed as the Indians watched a French engineer at Venango lay out a polygon 45 by 37 feet as the foundation of what later was named Fort Machault. The French brought mill machinery from Canada and set up a sawmill. They milled lumber which they would use the following year to construct 44 two-story houses to serve as a barracks, with a magazine 18 by 50 feet that would contain military stores protected from fire by a three-foot embankment.

"And what are the English doing?" demanded the Indians of their brother, the Buck. "Old Briton trusted you, and where is Old Briton? All you have is empty store houses and eleven families at Gist's."

Scurvy and dysentery gave the English some relief. Many Frenchmen died. Others were invalided home. Marin returned to Canada mortally ill. He left the command of Fort Le Boeuf to one-eyed Legardeur de St. Pierre and Venango to Joncaire.

The year 1754 was coming. The French would be back in greater force than ever. That was what St. Pierre and Joncaire promised the Indians. The French were going to protect their children, the red men, from the grasping English who always were greedy for more and more land.

The Indians were wavering in their allegiance in that fall of 1753. They would go with the English if they proved strength, but otherwise they would throw in with the French.

VII. *Into a Bleak Forest*

THE resolution of the French indicated to thinking frontiersmen that if the English meant to possess the Ohio, war
was inevitable. If war lay ahead, Washington meant to have
a hand in it. Not many months after Lawrence's death,
George took a few days off from surveying on the Fairfax
domain to ride to Williamsburg, where he reminded Governor
Dinwiddie that his brother had been adjutant of the Virginia
militia with the rank of major. The post was still vacant and
George asked for the appointment.

Dinwiddie put him off until he could confer with the council.
The councilmen demurred. Who was George Washington any-
how that he should ask for such a post? This 20-year-old
stripling had only a meager education. He had no military
experience, and except for 2000 acres of unimproved land, he
had no landed estate. Thumbs down on him!

Dinwiddie, with the council's advice, divided Virginia into
four military districts with an adjutant over each. To the three
more important districts, he named men of parts to serve as
adjutants. To the fourth district, that of southern Virginia,
bordering peaceful North Carolina, a district of no responsibility, he named Washington, giving him the relatively empty
title of major.

Swallowing disappointment, Washington engaged Jacob Van
Braam of Fredericksburg to instruct him in the manual of
arms, company drill, and swordsmanship. Van Braam was a

Dutch soldier of fortune, who, after various adventures, had served as a lieutenant in the War of Jenkins Ear. After that war, he settled at Fredericksburg where he tutored daughters of Virginia planters in atrocious French.

After that, when not surveying, George was fencing with Van Braam, studying military tactics, and practicing what he learned by drilling such squads as he could recruit in southern Virginia.

A year later, in October, 1753, while he was drilling 100 men at a colonial muster at Winchester, he heard the sneers of western men as they discussed how Trent and Russell had been frightened away from delivering Dinwiddie's ultimatum to the French commandant on the Ohio. The more Washington heard, the more he became convinced that he could succeed where others had failed.

Loyalty to England was doubtless a motive that impelled him. But there was more. He had been rejected by at least one girl's father as not worthy to marry a planter's daughter. When the Ohio Company had employed a surveyor, it went to North Carolina and hired Christopher Gist instead of Virginia's own. Then the council had declined to approve him as adjutant of northwest Virginia.

As has been related, he rode to Williamsburg and persuaded the governor to let him bear the ultimatum to the French. He left Williamsburg October 31. The weather must have been fine, for two days later he was already back at Fredericksburg, 113 dirt-road miles away. Here he persuaded Van Braam to accompany him as French interpreter. How could Washington, who knew no French, fathom the shallowness of Van Braam's understanding of that tongue?

Probably Washington paused for a brief visit with his mother at the old homestead just across the river. Then with Van Braam he rode to Alexandria, where he presented letters of credit from the governor with which he bought trade goods and wampum as gifts to the Indians. At Winchester he borrowed additional horses from Lord Fairfax.

Then he went to the Ohio Company's storehouse at Wills Creek. Here he met 47-year-old Gist, surveyor for the Ohio Company, a man ready for any hazard. Since Gist had tied his fortunes to those of the Ohio Company and had a new settlement near the Youghiogheny, he had a personal stake in Washington's venture. Washington delivered a letter from the governor, asking Gist to accompany Washington as lieutenant. Gist unhesitatingly agreed and helped Washington to engage four resourceful men, who could be relied upon in any circumstance. Two traders, who had traveled and traded extensively on the Ohio, were engaged as interpreters to the Indians. Two others, experienced in camp cooking, care of horses, and camp making, went as servitors.

The party of seven rode out of Wills Creek in the early morning of November 15. It required only a few horseback hours up the Narrows to bring them to the Divide, beyond which water flows no longer into the Potomac but westward into the Ohio. Here, beyond the influence of the Atlantic's tempering breezes, they found winter. Snow hissed through the naked branches of the trees. When it was not snowing, it was raining — a pelting, chilling rain.

By day the horses sloughed through the mud on the floor of the bleak forest. At nightfall the men hacked into dead trees for dry chips with which to kindle a fire on the sodden mast. They pitched a tent on the mire, cut boughs to lay on the floor of the tent, spread their blankets on the boughs, and all seven huddled together, while the cold horses browsed on twigs outside.

You may be sure they relished the change when they arrived at Frazier's rough hewn trading post at the mouth of Turtle

Creek, where they spent a night before the fireplace. From Frazier's they traveled to the Forks of the Ohio. There, as Washington stood at the point of land between the Monongahela and the Allegheny, he was struck with its strategic importance.

The grant of the Ohio Company provided that its land should lie on the south bank of the Ohio between the Monongahela and the Kanawha. It may be for that reason that Captain Trent, acting for the Ohio Company, had selected a site for a fort two miles farther downstream at the site of a Delaware village, whose chief was Shingiss. Washington saw no sense in choosing an inferior location merely because it was on the right side of the stream.

After crossing the Monongahela and journeying to the Shingiss village, he wrote in his journal: "I spent some time viewing the Rivers, and the Land in the Fork; which I think extremely well situated for a Fort, as it has absolute Command of both Rivers." Then, after commenting on his investigation of the Shingiss site, he added, "A Fort at the Forks would be equally well situated on the Ohio, and have the entire Command of the Monongahela; which runs up to our Settlements and is extremely well designed for water carriage."

While at the Delaware village Washington thought he had won the friendship of Shingiss, but it was a fickle friendship. The chief was a pacifist, but an enforced one. He was a Delaware, living on the Ohio, while the Delaware River, the natural home of his people, was on the eastern line of Pennsylvania, 290 miles to the East. Washington doubtless knew the story of the Delawares. Gist knew it, having been told it by the Indians themselves.

Shingiss accompanied Washington to Logstown, about 16 miles to the west on the Ohio River. This detour to the west when the French commandant was to the north was made at the express order of Dinwiddie. The governor had instructed Washington to visit the Indians, give them presents, and quench the distrust of the English that smoldered in the heart of nearly every Delaware.

The Delawares had been living a rich life in the Delaware Valley more than a century when pacifism was enforced upon them by the Iroquois Confederation, consisting of the Mohawks, Oneidas, Onondagas, Senecas, and Cayugas and later the Tuscaroras. Their villages extended from the Hudson River westward through New York to Niagara Falls. The Iroquois took satanic pleasure in torture and killing and journeyed far afield for no purpose other than to make enemies whom they might exterminate.

On one of their forays they swooped into the Delaware Valley of eastern Pennsylvania and western New Jersey to annihilate the people we call Delawares, but who named themselves the Leni-Lenape, meaning real people. The real people, knowing they would be destroyed if they relied on their hatchets, abjectly pleaded: "We are not warriors but women."

The Iroquois let them live on condition that they pay an annual tribute in beaver peltry and never make war on anybody, even in self-defense, without Iroquois permission.

Into this valley of enforced peace came a colony of Swedes, in 1638, who met the Delawares in council and bought a tract of land from them. They did not have to buy it, for the Delawares dared not fight, but they did it as a matter of right. The policy of buying land already had been established by the Dutch Reformed at what is now New York, by the Baptists of Rhode Island, the Congregationalists of Connecticut, and the Catholics of Maryland.

The Swedes raised the standard of living of the Delawares by bringing manufactured goods from Europe to trade for beaver furs, by teaching the Indians how to plow with horses and oxen, and by showing them how to build Swedish style log houses such as they later were to build at Logstown.

The Swedes lost their colony to the Dutch and later the English took over from the Dutch. Changes in government made no difference to the Delawares, for the Dutch and later the English continued the policy of paying for the land they occupied and of bringing manufactured goods to trade for beaver.

Approximately 6000 English, Dutch, and Swedes were living in what are now New Jersey, Delaware, and Pennsylvania in the valley of the Delaware by 1681. In that year King Charles II of England granted to William Penn a region with poorly defined borders, which roughly coincided with the present Pennsylvania.

William Penn was a man of benevolent and kindly character, but his kindliness worked to the disadvantage of the Delawares even though his intentions were of the best. He was a prominent member of the Society of Friends (Quakers), and designed his colony as a refuge for his coreligionists, who were persecuted in England. Since the Friends were pacifists, the situation was ideal for them, for the Delawares dared not fight. Further, they liked Penn and did not want to fight.

Penn, going further than merely providing a refuge for his own people, offered Pennsylvania as a haven for all mankind. He leased land at so trifling a rent that the very poorest could pay it. He required no military service, for he thought it a sin to fight. He tolerated every man, no matter what his religion. Colonists came by the tens of thousands not only from England but from the continent of Europe. Although eleven other of the thirteen colonies were founded earlier than Pennsylvania, his colony forged ahead and soon became most populous of them all.

The white settlers began crowding the Delawares, causing

them to move westward. It is true that Penn paid for the land, but he paid in perishable goods, which wore out while the land remained. Further, the Indians always were at a disadvantage in a real estate deal, no matter how well intentioned was the white man.

A sample of Penn's dealings is illustrated by what came to be called the Walking Treaty. By 1686 Penn foresaw the day when his rapidly growing colony would need more land. He negotiated a treaty by which the Delawares agreed to transfer all land, beginning at a sycamore tree at the junction of the Lehigh and Delaware rivers running northwest between the two streams to where it "doth extend itself back into the woods as far as a man can goe in a day and a half."

The treaty stipulated that the Indians need not vacate their lands until all the region south of the Lehigh should be settled. But Penn paid them immediately. It looked like such a good bargain that the Delawares signed willingly. Time passed. The area south of the Lehigh became settled. Many Delawares, finding that the settlers were killing their game, moved to the Forks of the Ohio and built several log villages, such as Logstown and Venango. Penn died. All the chiefs who had put their cross marks on the treaty died. The goods Penn had given wore out.

In 1730 William Penn's son Thomas, a non-Quaker who lived in England, ordered his agents in Pennsylvania to consummate the Walking Treaty. The Indians protested that they had forgotten the treaty or had never heard of it. They did, however, send witnesses to see how far a man can "goe in a day and a half."

They felt they were tricked because Penn's agents had cut a path through the forest to speed the walkers. Further they had chosen three walkers in competition to find the fastest men in the colony. They walked so rapidly from sunrise to sunset that the witnesses had to ride horseback to keep up. At night they rested, and the next morning one walker was so spent he could not stand up. After two hours of walking another dropped out. The third, Edward Marshall, walked until noon, reaching a point 66½ miles from the sycamore tree.

The Indians refused to leave their homes, and since the colony was founded on the theory of nonresistance, the agents could not evict them. After twelve years, Thomas Penn demanded that his agents do something. They, therefore, appealed to the Iroquois and presented them with gifts valued at £300. The Iroquois called the Delawares into council and told them: "You ought to be shaken by the hair of your heads!"

The helpless Delawares, driving their livestock before them, left their homes, their fields, and the graves of their fathers. Some moved just west of the treaty line. Some settled in the Wyoming Valley and some in the Susquehanna country. Others were swallowed into the defiles of the mountains and emerged to join their kinsmen on the Ohio, where they built more log towns. There by the fires they harangued each other concerning their wrongs and howled for vengeance.

But they did nothing more than howl. When the first Delawares moved into the Ohio region a part of the Iroquois followed them there. They lived in the Delaware villages and dominated their councils. The Delawares called the Ohio Iroquois the Mingoes, meaning the treacherous ones. But no matter what they called them, they were the actual rulers of the land, and Washington conferred more with the Mingoes at Logstown than he did with the Delawares.

He presented useful gifts and belts of wampum to show that he spoke with a straight tongue, and that his heart was right with his red brothers. He orated to them and they harangued back. Five days were consumed in powwows, but diplomatic courtesy of the forest required that he listen to every speech and ponder long before replying. The Indians had plenty of time. They did not have to dress for the opera or keep a business engagement. Present at the council were Delawares, Shawnees, Wyandottes, and Mingoes, each taking time for speeches and each expecting a long reply.

Shortly after his arrival at Logstown, a group of Frenchmen arrived from a Delaware village, Kuskuskung, a day's walk west of Logstown. Just how many there were is puzzling, for the journal relates: "Came to Town four or ten Frenchmen who had deserted from a Company at Kuskuskas, which lies at the Mouth of this River. . . . These deserters came up . . . with one Brown, an Indian Trader and were going to Philadelphia."

These Frenchmen revealed to Washington the immensity of the territory claimed by their country. Some had been at Vincennes on the Wabash. Some had visited Kaskaskia in the Illinois country. Their home was more than 1000 river miles away at New Orleans. They did not like military life, but when their king or governor told them to serve, they had to do it. From Brown they learned of the Friends idea of nonresistance and of the fact that nobody had to engage in military service in Pennsylvania unless he volunteered. And so they renounced France and became Pennsylvanians.

VIII. *Wily Diplomacy*

THE powwow with the Indians over, Washington prepared to execute the main phase of his mission. Several Indians insisted on accompanying him, because they wanted to see with their own eyes the delivery of the talking paper to the French.

Their chief man, Tanacharison, a 53-year-old Mingo, said he wanted to go along to protect the Virginians from the French. In Washington's journals this chief appears as Half King, so called because he was named to his post as headman on the Ohio by the Iroquois Council on the Mohawk and, therefore, was really a vassal and not a full king. Washington would have fared better without the Indians, but he could not tell an ally he was not wanted. From Logstown they journeyed to Venango, where over Frazier's blacksmith shop floated the lilies of France. Washington made his way to the shop and there met the commandant, Captain Thomas Philippe Joncaire.

The journal reports: "He invited us to sup with them; and treated us with the greatest Complaisance. The Wine, as they dosed themselves . . . gave license to their Tongues to reveal their Sentiments more freely. They told me, That it was their Absolute Design to take Possession of the Ohio, and by G— they would do it: for altho' they were sensible the English could raise two Men to their one; yet they knew their Motions were too slow and dilatory to prevent any Undertaking of theirs."

Taking the measure of the messenger, the half-breed Joncaire could not help but notice that he was the youngest of the seven yet in command. Washington demanded to know why they had driven Frazier from his blacksmith shop and trading store. To this Joncaire answered with evident satisfaction that Frazier was lucky to have escaped. The land belonged to France by virtue of its discovery by La Salle, so he said.

When Washington presented the ultimatum from Dinwiddie, Joncaire explained that he was merely the commandant at Venango. He directed Washington, therefore, to go to a superior officer at Fort Le Boeuf. It was three days, however, before Washington could go on, for Joncaire treated the Indians to liquor. Half King was loathe to leave the jug, and Washington did not want to abandon him to the influence of the Frenchman. At length he sobered Half King, and the journey was resumed.

Joncaire assigned Captain La Force, a suave commissary officer, to command an escort that would accompany the Virginia emissary to Le Boeuf.

The journey continued through rain and snow. On December 12 they were at Le Boeuf. Washington met the one-eyed commander, Captain Le Gardeur de St. Pierre de Repentigny, who understood a little English, and, with Van Braam's blundering help, managed to make enough of a translation of Dinwiddie's message for him to understand its import. St. Pierre proposed that Washington carry the message to Quebec, but the major realized that when he arrived there he might be directed to go to Paris. He insisted that his governor had directed him to the highest commanding officer on the Ohio, and he demanded an answer.

As St. Pierre and Van Braam struggled with the translation, Washington and Gist took a turn about Le Boeuf. The major set down in his journal the dimensions and strength of the fort, the number of men garrisoned there, and the number of

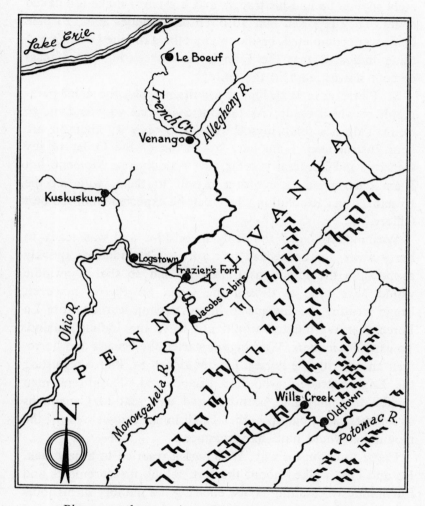

Places on the way from Virginia to Fort Le Boeuf

boats and canoes in building. Not wishing to be caught deliberately spying, he had his traders and horsemen make a detailed
count. They reported that 50 birch bark canoes and 170 pine
boats were completed, besides many others roughed out. Everything indicated that the French were preparing for a mass
descent downstream in the spring.

St. Pierre gave Washington a written reply, the chief para-
graph of which read: "As to your Summons you send me to
retire, I do not think myself obliged to obey it; whatever are
your Instructions, I am here by Virtue of the Order of my
General; and I entreat you Sir, not to doubt one Moment, but
I am determined to conform myself to them, with all the
Exactness and Resolution which can be expected from the best
Officer."

Washington folded the reply in oilskins and was ready to
hurry away, for he needed to report to Dinwiddie as quickly
as possible the intentions of the French so that Dinwiddie
would have time to defend the Ohio. St. Pierre, however,
began treating the Indians to liquor, having learned from La
Force that Washington would not leave the Indians behind.
To expedite matters, Washington started the traders and horsemen ahead with the horses. He questioned St. Pierre regarding
the English traders who had disappeared. The Frenchman
replied that they had been arrested and sent to Canada as
trespassers, and that any other Englishman caught west of the
mountains would have like treatment.

Eager to be on his way, Washington resorted to a new tack.
He and Gist walked about the fort, taking measurements and
ostentatiously counting boats, entering the number in his jour-
nal. St. Pierre thought it better to get rid of him and directed
La Force to make ready canoes and escort the English and
Indians back to Venango.

A wild voyage ensued, as Washington wrote: "Several Times

we were like to have been staved against Rocks; and many Times were obliged all Hands get out and remain in the Water Half an Hour or more, getting over Shoals."

At Venango La Force and Washington, having endured privation together, parted ostensibly as friends. How could they know as they clasped hands that in five short months they would be striving to kill each other from opposite sides of the firing line? Washington regretfully left the Indians at Venango. One of them fell seriously ill, and Half King would not leave him. He promised Washington, however, that he would not let the fork-tongued Joncaire separate him from his love for the English.

The horses were by this time too weak even to carry the baggage. Their steps were so faltering that they were delaying the return to Virginia. Washington and Gist, therefore, placed Van Braam in command of the traders and servitors with instructions to bring the horses as rapidly as they could. Many weeks later they arrived at Winchester, turning back to Lord Fairfax and others the animals that had survived. They had started out in good condition but were now stumbling and decrepit nags.

Washington and Gist spent Christmas Eve and Christmas night in the snow without shelter, for they had given the tent to those who would be longer on the trail and needed it more. "I took my necessary Papers," wrote Washington, "pulled off my Cloaths; and tied myself up in a Match Coat, Then with Gun in Hand and Pack at my Back, in which were my Papers and Provisions, I set out with Mr. Gist, fitted in the same Manner."

As they stalked through the timber, Washington and Gist speculated on the possibility of meeting Indians in the French interest. Shortly after they had left Venango, they saw four canoe loads of Frenchmen pass down the Allegheny. Were they sent to induce the Indians to waylay and kill the messengers so as to prevent a report to Dinwiddie? They thought so, and their suspicions were confirmed a few days later when they were joined by an Indian, carrying a musket loaded and primed with the flint set. He offered to guide them, explaining that with his aid they would avoid Indians favorable to the French. He even persuaded Washington to give up his pack, which the Indian slung over a shoulder. He also offered to carry Washington's gun, but the major declined.

As they proceeded, Gist noticed that the Indian was leading them out of their course and protested. Whatever were the motives of the Indian, we can but conjecture from what he did. Perhaps he was trying to lead them into ambush. When he failed because of Gist's alertness, he apparently decided to kill the two men, carry off their packs and scalps, and claim a reward. Knowing himself to be fleet of foot and figuring any fast Indian could outrun any white man, he felt he was safe in firing the load in his gun to kill one of the men. He expected he could escape by running before the other could prime his firing pan. Then he could take his time to waylay and kill the other.

At a distance of only fifteen paces, he rammed the butt of his weapon to his shoulder, aimed, and squeezed the trigger. The flint sparked. The powder flashed. The bullet screeched. Amazing as it may seem, he missed. He darted off, paused behind a tree, and began to reload. The white men gave him no time. In a moment the fleetest foot racer of Virginia and the rugged Gist were upon him. After a short tussle, he gave up. Gist was for killing him, but Washington vetoed the proposal. They kept the Indian with them until 9 o'clock at night, when they released him. After that, so Washington's journal relates: "[We] walked all the remaining Part of the Night without making any Stop; that we might get the start, so far, as to be out of the Reach of their Pursuit the next Day, since we were well assured they would follow our Tract as soon as it was light."

The next day they continued and came to the banks of the Allegheny River in the outskirts of the present Pittsburgh. The river was frozen only about 50 yards out from the shore. They, therefore, slept on the bank that night. The next day, from daylight to dark, they built a raft. For this work they had only one poor hatchet.

As dusk came they launched their jerry-built craft and tried to steer it with poles. The current was stronger than they had calculated. Floes of ice crashed downstream. They narrowly averted collision after collision. Their crazy raft, caught in the swirl of the current, went careening toward a cake of ice. When Washington attempted to check the impact with his pole, a gyration of the water brought raft and floe together despite all he could do. He clung to the pole, and in his effort to retain it, was hurled into the icy water. "I fortunately saved myself by catching hold of one of the Raft Logs," related Washington. "Notwithstanding all our efforts we could not get the Raft to either Shore; but were obliged, as we were near an Island to quit our Raft and make to it."

Here the castaways spent a night in anxiety and cold. Their clothing was sheathed in ice. The night became colder and colder. Not at any other time on their journey had it been so cold. Washington's narrative says: "The Cold was so extremely severe, that Mr. Gist had all his Fingers, and some of his Toes frozen. But when morning came, the water was shut up so hard, that we found no Difficulty in getting-off the Island, on the ice."

They came to shore at what is now Washington's Crossing Bridge in Pittsburgh. Shelter was twelve miles away. At the mouth of Turtle Creek they stumbled into Frazier's friendly headquarters and thawed their clothing before his fireplace.

Frazier told Washington that he had given offense to Queen Aliquippa, a Delaware chieftainess, because he had not called on her as he passed that way before. She lived only a few miles away, and so Washington, doing what he could to retain the good will of the Indians, paid her a visit. His report to Dinwiddie, records: "I made her a Present of a Matchcoat and a Bottle of Rum, which latter was thought much the best Present of the Two."

The matchcoat was so named because it was of matched furs. The English made imitation matchcoats of wool. Since Aliquippa had all the furs she needed, it is probable that Washington presented her a warm woolen coat.

At Frazier's house Washington encountered 20 Indians, who had been on a hunt as far as the head of the Great Kanawha River. Here lived several families of Virginia pioneers, who had pushed into the forest beyond the lands claimed by Lord Fairfax and beyond the travels of the tax or rent collectors. The price for their free life came high. Washington's journal set forth: "They [the Indians] found seven people killed and scalped (all but one woman with very light hair). They turned about and ran back for fear the inhabitants should rise and take them as the authors of the murder. They reported that the bodies were lying about the house, and some of them much torn and eaten by hogs. By the marks which were left, they say they were French Indians of the Ottaway Nation, &c., who did it."

The call on Aliquippa ended and the story of the Indians recorded, Washington and Gist moved on to Jacobs Cabins on Jacobs Creek, which flows into the Youghiogheny. There they spent the night. Captain Jacobs was an English-speaking Delaware Indian, who had spent his youth and early manhood east of the mountains. He had withdrawn from the encroaching

Pennsylvanians. Ostensibly, he was friendly to the English, but it took more than a Virginian to read the mind back of the captain's inscrutable eyes.

The next night the travelers spent at Gist's new settlement across the river and several miles beyond Jacobs Cabins. There Washington obtained a horse and saddle and left Gist to nurse his frostbitten toes. He expected to ride through a solitude, but just west of the Narrows, he encountered Captain Trent, leading a party of Virginia volunteers with tools and provisions loaded on seventeen pack horses. Dinwiddie was trusting Trent a second time. He was now sent to build a fort on the Ohio. Washington does not say so, but he must have given Trent his plans for placing the fort at the Forks of the Ohio, for that is where Trent built, naming the rude log structure Fort George.

The day after encountering Trent, Washington met families on their way to Gist's settlement. Men, women, and children, defying what Washington described as "excessively bad weather," were going out in the winter so that they could build their log homes before spring. That would leave them free to plant corn as soon as the oak leaves were as long as squirrel's ears.

Washington lost no time at Wills Creek. He did rest one day with William Fairfax at Belvoir. This man had a liking for Washington and was ever a friend and counselor. Leaving Belvoir, Washington reported to Dinwiddie at Williamsburg on January 16, presenting him with the journal of his mission, concluding with: "I hope what has been said will be sufficient to make your Honour satisfied with my Conduct, for that was my Aim in undertaking the Journey, and chief Study throughout the Prosecution of it."

IX. *Too Little, Too Late*

FOR accepting the risks he ran on his journey to Fort Le Boeuf, Washington won immediate rewards. He learned from Dinwiddie that during his absence he had been appointed to the coveted post of major of northwest Virginia. It was satisfying to learn that this honor and responsibility came, not because he belonged to a distinguished family, but because he had earned it.

More rewards were on the way. Members of the Council now went out of their way to be seen in his company. John Robinson, speaker of the House of Burgesses, was so impressed with Washington's exploit that he became his friend. No sunshine friend was he. In the tragic months to come, when others turned away, Robinson was ever Washington's champion in the Virginia capital. Of course, since Washington had volunteered his services on his mission to Le Boeuf, he expected no pay, but the next meeting of the Burgesses voted him a reward of £50.

Armed with Washington's journal, the governor now planned a campaign to sell the Burgesses on the necessity of voting men and money for defense. He had tried it in November after Washington had left on his mission to warn the French out of the Ohio. At that time he had summoned the Burgesses into session and warned them that it would be necessary to meet force with force.

Instead of voting the money, the Burgesses spent their time attacking the governor for collecting taxes, which they held were unauthorized. In a memorial they declared: "The rights of the subjects are secured by law that they cannot be deprived of the least part of their property but by their own consent."

One tax they resented was a fee of one pistole that Dinwiddie charged for signing a patent to a tract of land. He contended it was a charge for services performed and not a tax. Anyway, he used the money for the expenses of his position. Neither side would yield. When the Burgesses insisted that they would not vote money for defense until he agreed to rescind the pistole tax, he prorogued the House.

Now, as he read Washington's journal and came to the place where Washington related how Joncaire had sneered that the English are too slow to win the Ohio, he must have devoutly wished for absolute authority like that of the ruler of Canada. There the French governor issued edicts, collected taxes, and ordered out the militia without backtalk.

Dinwiddie hired the journal printed, sent copies to the Councilmen, the Lords of Trade in London, and the Burgesses, and called the Burgesses back to meet on February 15. He told the Burgesses that the king already had sent cannon, other munitions, and money and that the other colonies were voting help. Now he wanted the Burgesses to vote a regiment of 600 men and £20,000. In his address to the Burgesses he shouted a warning as he retold the account in Washington's journal of the killing of seven frontiersmen on the Great Kanawha.

"Think," the governor exhorted, "you see the Infant torn from the unavailing Struggles of the distracted mother, the daughters ravished before the eyes of their wretched Parents, and then with Cruelty and Insult, butcher'd and scalp'd. Suppose the horrid Scene compleated and the whole Family, Man, Wife and Children (as they were) murdered and Scalp'd by these relentless Savages and then torn in Pieces, and in Part devour'd by wild Beasts, for whom they were left a Prey by their more brutal Enemies. But how must your Indignation rise when you extend your View to the Abbetors of these Villanies.

"Such are the People whose Neighborhood you must now prevent, or with the most probable Expectation Think to see in the Bosom of Your Country these Evils that You as yet only have the melancholy Tidings of from Your Frontier."

The Burgesses were stirred, but not enough. A minority argued that Dinwiddie must first renounce his right to collect the pistole tax. Some contended that the Ohio was the property of Pennsylvania and that colony should defend it. Some brought out that Dinwiddie's zeal was caused by the fact that he was a stockholder in the Ohio Company. Let the Ohio Company pay the bill. This last charge was unjust. In his lifetime of government service, the governor never had used his position for personal gain. Further, the king's long delay in granting a charter to the Ohio Company had allowed the French to gain a position too strong for a mere company to cope with the situation. Even Virginia was not strong enough now. Other colonies must help.

While the minority bickered, the majority of the Burgesses, led by Speaker Robinson, voted £10,000 instead of the requested £20,000. It was too little to equip and supply 600 men and too little to buy presents for the Indians. Dinwiddie swallowed his chagrin. He wrote to the governors of other colonies exaggerating what Virginia was doing and imploring them to do as much as he said Virginia had voted. It was a trick he had to stir others to emulate Virginia. He also exaggerated to the Virginians what other colonies were doing. The Burgesses enraged Dinwiddie by naming a committee to supervise the governor's spending of the money voted for defense. Exasperated he wrote to the Lords of Trade: "They have clogged it with unreasonable regulat's and Encroachm'ts."

The governor would have liked to draft the able bodied men from 18 to 45 years old into the service, but he could gain no co-operation. It was illegal to send the militia outside the colony, and many Virginians contended that the Ohio was outside of Virginia.

Dinwiddie appointed Joshua Fry, a respected gentleman with no combat experience, as colonel of Virginia. Fry was a surveyor and engineer who had taught mathematics at William and Mary College. He had studied military drill, and his appointment met favor.

A second honor came to Washington at about his twenty-second birthday. He was named lieutenant colonel. John Carlyle, a son-in-law of William Fairfax, was named major in charge of the commissary. He was directed to buy flour, salt pork, beeves on the hoof, and other provisions. Ten of the king's cannon Carlyle was to transport by sloop to the Falls of the Potomac, thence by wagons to Wills Creek, where the Ohio Company storehouse would serve as a supply depot. Wagons and horses he was to buy where he could get them. The king had sent 200 muzzle-loading rifles, the most modern in the world of that time. Hampered by a shortage of money, Carlyle at no time was able to supply adequate provisions. He had authority to impress wagons, but farmers hid them, and local authorities would not inform on their neighbors.

Washington was instructed to enroll 100 recruits in Augusta and Frederick counties, west of the Blue Ridge. Fry, with headquarters at Alexandria, was to enroll 350 from all the rest of Virginia. Trent was to find 100 recruits among the traders and to get help from the Mingoes, Delawares, Shawnees, and Wyandottes. In his instructions to Trent, Dinwiddie referred to the French as "certain persons pretending to be subjects of his most christian majesty the king of France." Since England and France were at peace, it would not do to fight Frenchmen, but it was all right to fight "certain persons pretending to be subjects."

Trent was further instructed "to dislodge and drive away, and in case of refusal and resistance to Kill and destroy or take prisoners all and every person and persons not subjects of the King of Great Britain who now or hereafter come to settle and take possession of any Lands on said River Ohio or any of the Brooks or Waters Thereof." Similar clear instructions were later given to Washington. Critics who have condemned Washington for starting an undeclared war have overlooked reading the instructions.

Besides asking for troops from Virginia and the other colonies, Dinwiddie directed Trent to negotiate with all of the Ohio Indians. He also sent emissaries to the Catawabas, Cherokees, and Chickasaws to recruit 1000 warriors.

The plan was all right, but it was not implemented with enough money. On March 9 Washington lamented to Dinwiddie that he had enrolled only 25 recruits and they were from the riffraff — men with no shoes, no stockings, no shirts, no waistcoats. No tobacco had come to pay them. Tobacco was the common currency of Virginia. While they talked of pounds, shillings, and pence, the common people rarely saw coins other than occasional Spanish doubloons and pistoles. The men he had enrolled could not be sent out in cold weather for lack of clothing. "You may, with equal success, attempt to raise the dead to life again," commented Washington.

Dinwiddie responded with a new tack. He offered 200,000 acres of land on the Ohio to be divided among the volunteers, who, after the defeat of the French, could occupy the part allotted to them free of quit rents for 15 years. It was a good stroke. In a few days after the announcement, Washington had 159 men under arms. Colonel Fry had 100 and Trent had 70.

Trent, unfortunately, saw a chance to make money in the

fur trade. He was often absent from Fort George and others followed his example. He asked Dinwiddie to commission Frazier as lieutenant and Edward Ward as ensign. Since Frazier had a trading post to care for, he, too, was absent from the fort most of the time. The command, therefore, devolved on Ward, who struggled with building the fort. For the most part his men were Pennsylvania traders and not Virginians, but since Pennsylvania was a pacifist state and since the traders had a personal stake in the contest, they took service where it would be accepted.

In April Dinwiddie directed Washington to proceed to the Forks of the Ohio and take command. He was to move his supplies rapidly by pack horse. Fry was to come later and cut a wagon road through the forest so that cannon could be moved up. For fresh beef, Washington was to receive from Carlyle a herd of cattle which would be driven along to be butchered as needed.

Washington was already too late. As he was marching from Winchester toward the crossing of the Potomac at Cresap's Oldtown, he received an express from Trent imploring aid. He had been informed by the Indians that a French expedition was on the way down the Allegheny.

The expedition, headed by Pierre de Contrecoeur, had come from Montreal with the breakup of ice. From Presque Isle Contrecoeur portaged to Le Boeuf where St. Pierre had completed production of 60 batteaux and 300 canoes and boats. On the crest of a spring freshet they bounded down French Creek to Venango and there added Joncaire's force to the expedition.

Eight hundred strong, the men sang roundelays as they rode the Allegheny to a point two miles above Fort George. There they beached their boats and threw out a cordon of men from the Allegheny to the Monongahela to cut off escape by land.

Downhill they marched to the fort at the Forks where they found Ward in command. Even in the face of emergency Trent was absent. Ward's men threw down axes and bars to grab weapons, but Contrecoeur signaled for a parley. All he asked was that Ward pack his tools and other property on his horses and move out. He gave him until 2 p.m. the next day.

Since Ward had only 41 men of whom 33 were soldiers, and since Contrecoeur had 800 together with 18 cannon, besides a flotilla to bring more men and supplies from Canada, Ward knew he could not win, even though he might hold out for a few days and kill some of the Frenchmen. He called a council of his men, who voted to accept the terms offered.

On April 17, while Washington was still on the way to Oldtown, Ward marched out of the unfinished fort. He had gone but a short distance when he was overtaken in the woods by Half King and a group of other warriors from Logstown. Ward explained that the English were coming back in great force. Half King wanted to know if this was just more big English talk. To make sure he assigned two Indians to go with Ward and count the English. He also delivered to the Indians three speeches, one for Washington, one for Dinwiddie, and one for Governor James Hamilton of Pennsylvania.

Washington began meeting refugees at Oldtown, including traders from the Ohio and families from Gist's settlement. At Wills Creek he met Ward himself and Half King's two Indians. Even before Ward could relate the details of his surrender, one of the Indians interrupted and recited the message from Half King, which closed with: "If you do not come to our assistance now, we are entirely undone, and I think we shall never meet together again. I speak with a heart full of grief."*

---

* Quotations from Dinwiddie are taken from R. A. Brock, ed., *The Official Records of Robert Dinwiddie, 1751–1758,* in the Collections of the Virginia Historical Society, Richmond, 1883. Quotations from Half King are from Sparks, *The Writings of Washington.*

X. *The First Road West*

SINCE it no longer was sensible to proceed to the Forks of the Ohio with so small a force, Washington called a council of officers to evolve a new plan. The council agreed to advance slowly, hewing a road as they advanced, to enable the main part of the regiment under Colonel Fry to catch up.

Washington directed Ward to report the details of the loss of Fort George to Dinwiddie in person. One Indian accompanied Ward so that he could learn from the governor's own mouth how much the English loved the Indians and how Dinwiddie was sending an army to protect them from the French. The rest of Ward's force was incorporated into Washington's command, but a number deserted.

Washington took time to write detailed letters to Dinwiddie, to Governor Hamilton of Pennsylvania, and to Colonel Fry, explaining that they were building a road to the Ohio Company storehouse at Redstone at the mouth of Redstone Creek. That was a good place to establish a base from which to launch an expedition by boats against the French at the Forks, which was but 37 miles farther down the river.

He also wrote a reply to Half King, signing it Conotocarious, meaning Devourer of Villages, a title the Virginia Indians had conferred upon the first Washington in America. He read it to the Mingo messenger so that he could memorize it and recite it to Half King. In the letter Washington asked Half King to bring his warriors to unite with the English.

Up through the Narrows from Wills Creek Washington's

men hewed a road. Across the Divide they moved into a region where rainwater flows west to the Ohio. Heretofore, all trails beyond the Divide had been mere pathways for men afoot or ahorse to follow single file. Washington was building a road — the first road into the West.

Early every morning the crack, crack, crack, of axes biting into wood disturbed the squirrels. As the axmen felled a tree, other men with axes and pike poles lopped off the branches and rolled the tree trunks and limbs out of the roadway. Stumps were left, but they chopped them low enough to clear wagon axles. Then came the earth movers with picks and shovels to grade the roadway. It was arduous work. When the column arrived at the first crossing of the Youghiogheny River, Washington surveyed that stream to see if it would not be feasible to take to boats from that point. But after a voyage of a few miles, in which his craft was stove in by hidden rocks, and he encountered other embarrassment, he abandoned the idea as impracticable and continued cutting toward Red-stone, following the best grades. Eminent engineers with the most modern surveying instruments followed almost the same grade as they laid out the present U. S. Highway 40.

Considering that every bit of roadway was constructed by hand tools, the progress was remarkably swift. It was April 27 when the column left Wills Creek. By May 20 the road was complete to Turkey Track, where Laurel Hill Creek, Castleman's River, and the Youghiogheny come together like three toes of a turkey's foot. Six miles more brought them to the Great Meadows, great only in comparison with the Little Meadows, which the column had already passed.

Before the coming of the white man with his carelessness at campfires, nature grew trees all the way from Wills Creek to the Great Lakes and hundreds of miles beyond. Now and then a tree, thrusting its conceited crown above its fellows, became a target for lightning, which sometimes scarred the timber giants, sometimes struck them prostrate, and sometimes set them afire. Fires spread, leaving nothing but the blackened snags of trees to molder into dust. As a balm for the burn, nature spread a mantle of grass, and the area remained a meadow, until shrubs and trees once more reclaimed the realm of the forest.

On the Great Meadows deer grazed. Here, too, because of the sunlight, songbirds built their nests and sang. Perhaps in the forgotten past, an Indian war band may have come to the Great Meadows, but as far as history recalls, this was the first military party to pass that way. The commands of the officers, the creaking of the wagons, the bite of ax into wood, the crash of falling timber startled awake the echoes which had slept in peace in the adjoining hills since unremembered years.

Washington noted that the Great Meadows afforded lush grass for the horses and cattle. He also decided that an army might make a stand here, for no enemy could approach without being seen. A branch of Meadows Run, which drains the glade, afforded fresh water for cattle and men. Two dry ditches, which drained into the run in time of rain, could serve as entrenchments. All in all the Great Meadows was from 200 to 400 yards wide and two and a half miles long. To Dinwiddie, Washington wrote: "A charming place for an encounter."

At a point about 100 yards from a forested hill on one side and 150 yards to a forested hill on the other, he stepped off the outlines of a fort, naming it Fort Necessity. He set some of the men to building the fort, while others continued extending the road toward Redstone. He was still at the Great Meadows when Ward arrived, bearing a letter from Dinwiddie, complimenting Washington and his officers for cutting the road. The letter was full of promises.

Colonel Fry was at Winchester, so Dinwiddie wrote. Actually, he was still recruiting volunteers at Alexandria. The governor reported that his personal friend, Colonel James Innes of North Carolina, was on his way with 350 men, for whose support the North Carolina legislature had voted £12,000. Captain James Mackay of South Carolina had arrived in Virginia with 100 men and 100 more were coming. Maryland was sending 200 men and so was New York. Actually Maryland sent none. Washington looked wistfully backward up the road he had built, but there was no sign of Colonel Fry.

In addition to his other duties, Washington had to double as chaplain. If a man died, the colonel read the funeral service from an Anglican prayer book. On Sundays he doubled as chaplain again. The thought that he ought to conduct services came from William Fairfax, who wrote Washington: "I will not doubt your having public prayers in the camp, especially when the Indian families are your guests, that they, seeing your plain manner of worship, may have their curiosity excited to be informed why we do not use the ceremonies of the French, which being well explained to their understandings will more and more dispose them to receive our baptism, and unite in strict bonds of cordial friendship."*

Occasionally Indians arrived from Logstown. The same Indians visited the French at the Forks and carried news from one side to the other. Yet they had to be treated with respect. They told the French that Washington had only 190 men less a dozen deserters.

On Washington's part he learned that Contrecoeur, disdaining Fort George, tore it down to replace it with a larger fort, naming it Duquesne for the governor of Canada. The fort was of squared logs in the form of a triangle. The French packed

* The letter from William Fairfax is from Sparks, *The Writings of Washington.*

its base with a 12-foot thick earthen embankment. Contrecoeur's men had built a stockade in front of the fort from
river to river and were clearing the forest for a half mile in
front of the fort to provide clear vision in case of an enemy
approach. In the clearing the Frenchmen were planting corn,
wheat, and vegetables to provide fresh green food to fend off
scurvy.

Washington also learned that the French were sending an
expedition to attack him. The first definite news he had of
this came from Half King, penned by John Davison who had
been one of Washington's companions on the journey to Le
Boeuf the previous December. His letter read: "To the forist,
His Majesties Commander Offiverses to hom this meay concern,
On acc't of a Freench armey to meat Miger George Wassiontton
therefore my Brotheres I deesir you to be awar of them for
deisin'd to strik ye forist English they see ten days since they
marchd I cannot tell what nomber the half-King and the rest of
the Chiefs will be with you in five days to consel, no more
at present but give my serves to my Brothers the English."

Additional news came from Christopher Gist. A French
and Indian detachment had stopped at Gist's settlement, twelve
miles northwest of Fort Necessity, and the Frenchmen had
prepared to kill one of Gist's cows. The Indians, however,
protested that Gist was their friend. Rather than offend the
Indians the French spared the cow and went toward Washington's camp. On May 27 Gist, having been summoned to attend a war council called by Governor Dinwiddie at Winchester,
rode by the Great Meadows and told of the near presence of the
Frenchmen, but could not tell where they were hiding. He
estimated that there were 50 in the party.

XI. *The Bullets Whistle*

THE night after Gist had gone toward Winchester, a Mingo runner, Silverheels, came to Washington with a message from Half King who was encamped just a few miles away. The Mingoes, so Silverheels reported, had come on the tracks of two Frenchmen who had disappeared into a secluded part of the forest.

His men already were going to bed, but Washington selected 40 as athletic as himself, with Lieutenant Van Braam and Captain Thomas Waggoner from among the officers. Directing the rest of his force to guard the wagons, horses, and military stores, he set out into the dark, guided by Silverheels. Soon they were entangled in a laurel thicket. Rain subdued the fragrance of the pink and white laurel blossoms now in full bloom.

"My men set out in a heavy rain," noted Washington, "and in a night as dark as pitch along a path scarce broad enough for one man; we were sometimes fifteen or twenty minutes out of the path before we could come to it again, and we would often strike each other in the darkness: All night long we continued our route, and on the 28th about sun-rise we arrived at the Indian camp."

A bedraggled, hungry lot stumbled into Half King's camp with seven men strayed and lost in the laurel thickets. Half King had but a dozen Mingo and Delaware warriors. Washington, having lost seven, had only 33, a total of 45 men. And yet Half King and Washington decided to track the Frenchmen to their hiding place, surround them, and take them prisoners.

And there were supposed to be 50 French and Indians! Washington did not know it, but the Indians had withdrawn and the French numbered 34. Even at that, it was a bold decision. Following two expert Indian trackers, the column marched

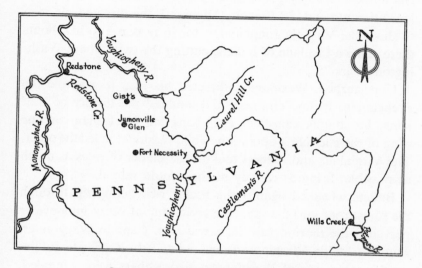

Scene of Washington's early battles

single file with Washington on the heels of the trackers. It never occurred to the lieutenant colonel that Half King might lead him into ambush. Washington remembered that in the previous December the Mingo chief had promised at Venango to continue to love the English. His recent communications confirmed that idea.

The French boot tracks led to a depressed glen, rimmed round with rock. It was a perfect hiding place. Breakfast fires were burning, but their reflections were absorbed by the dense overhanging foliage. Washington did not see the camp until his figure was silhouetted on the rimrock. Both parties saw each other at about the same instant. Washington saw the

Frenchmen throw down eating utensils, grab up guns, and dash for the protection of the rocks.

Among the Frenchmen he recognized his comrade of the journey from Venango to Le Boeuf — Captain La Force. His mask of suavity gone, he was now a hateful enemy barking out commands in French. Apparently he directed his men to shoot the Virginia commander, for in response to his shouts there came a fusillade of bullets, cutting the twigs about Washington's ears.

Unperturbed, Washington directed his men to encircle the Frenchmen. If any Virginian had doubted the loyalty of Half King, his doubts vanished. Half King led his Indians at one wing of the encircling operation, while Washington led the other. The Virginians and Indians took to the shelter of trees as much as possible, firing as rapidly as they could reload.

Bullets whacked against the rocks, ricocheting up through the forest roof into the sky. The acrid tang of burnt gunpowder pervaded the morning air. This was war. Captain Waggonner, standing beside Washington, was wounded. A private soldier on the other side of Washington died. Others were wounded. The Virginians and their Indian allies had by this time completed their encircling movement, which not only cut off the French retreat, but exposed the rear of those men firing from behind rocks.

The attackers, firing from all sides, rested their gun barrels against trees and aimed to kill. Ten Frenchmen died, among them Captain Joseph Coulon de Jumonville, who outranked Le Force and was theoretically in command. Half King bounded from cover to rip off Jumonville's scalp.

"There were 5 or 6 Indians who served to knock the poor, unhappy wounded in the head, and bereiv'd them of their scalps," Washington related to Dinwiddie. "So that we had but 40 men with which we tried and took 32 or 3 men, besides others, who may have escaped."

The battle lasted 15 minutes when La Force, with one half of his men dead or wounded, cried for quarter. Washington was accepting his submission, when Half King came running up with brandished club to strike La Force. Washington fended him away, explaining that the living Frenchmen, even the wounded, were now prisoners, and it was unchivalrous to kill a prisoner. What strange ideas these white men had!

Speaking through Van Braam as interpreter, La Force protested that he was an emissary and entitled to all the courtesies that had been shown Washington on his journey to Le Boeuf. Washington, however, gave no credence to the tale. Ambassadors did not lurk in the woods for days. He detached 20 men to escort the prisoners to Williamsburg. He could ill spare the escort, but he had captured two French captains, two cadets, and seventeen privates and it took 20 men to guard them. Two Frenchmen had escaped, running barefoot before the encircling movement was completed. One was caught and killed by a party of Mingoes not connected with Washington's camp. The other, his feet bloody and bruised, reached Fort Duquesne, to tell of the battle. Washington had lost one killed and a few slightly wounded. To his brother Jack, he wrote: "I fortunately escaped without any wound, for the right wing, where I stood, was exposed to and received all the enemy's fire, and it was the part where the man was killed and the rest wounded. I heard the bullets whistle, and, believe me, there is something charming in the sound."

Eventually Jack's letter was printed in the *London Magazine,* and reached the eye of King George, who chuckled derisively and remarked that Washington had had little experience with bullets, or he would not have thought them "something charming." Horatio Walpole, Earl of Oxford and famed wit, called Washington a braggart, but the exploit thrilled London. In Virginia men talked of little else. Planters sent their slaves to importune travelers on the roads to stop and dine and spend the night and relate any news they had of Washington.

The battle bolstered Washington's confidence. He had proved to himself that he could stand unflinching in time of deadly peril. He expressed this confidence several weeks later, when confronted with overwhelming odds, by writing to Dinwiddie: "If you hear that I am beaten, you will, at the same time, hear that we have done our duty, in fighting as long as there was a possibility of hope."

Among the Indians a legend was born. Had not Washington, coming home from Le Boeuf, been fired upon at a distance of only fifteen paces and escaped unhit? Had not he been exposed at Jumonville Glen to the mass fire of the Frenchmen and all bullets had missed? Surely he was big medicine!

The Indians admired the colonel, but he had no presents. And so, after counting the number of French at Fort Duquesne and the number of English with Washington, most of them prudently picked the one they felt would win.

Dinwiddie, trying to help Washington, ordered Fry to move. To Washington the governor wrote: "You cannot believe the Uneasiness and Anxiety I have had for the Tardiness of the Detachm't under Colo Fry's co'd in not joining You some Time since. Continue in good Spirits and prosecute Y'r usual Conduct and Prudence wich must recomend Yo to the favo. of His M'y and Y'r Country."

Poor Colonel Fry, his reputation as a scholar was of no help when on a horse. His mount threw him, and his injuries confined him to his quarters. Instead of ordering his next in command, Major George Muse, to reinforce Washington, he lay abed, neither exercising authority nor relinquishing it. He did not last long. When he died of his injuries, Dinwiddie dispatched an order to Muse to join Washington at once. He also commissioned Muse as lieutenant colonel. Muse was older than Washington and a veteran of the War of Jenkins Ear, but Dinwiddie, measuring the two men, commissioned Washington as a full colonel and named him commander of all Virginia troops raised or to be raised.

Half King and Queen Aliquippa brought 25 armed Mingoes and Delawares to Washington's standard. They also brought 55 women and children for Washington to feed. Muse arrived soon after with 189 men and nine cannon mounted on swivels. They brought an inadequate supply of bacon and flour and drove a few cattle to be butchered for fresh beef.

Muse also brought several minor officers who were to be with Washington a long time and some who would soon be lost as companions. Among these was 27-year-old Robert Stobo, who had come from Scotland to represent his father as buyer of tobacco and seller of Scotch manufactured goods. Fascinated with the thought of adventure and a trip to the Ohio, Stobo obtained a captain's commission from Dinwiddie. With his own funds he bought supplies for his men and a wagon to haul the freight. To the supplies he added a cask of Madeira wine and made himself popular with everybody.

Another of Muse's men was Andrew Montour, whose father was an Oneida chief and whose mother was half Huron and half French. He rated himself a white man and English and as such had engaged in the Ohio fur trade. An account relates: "He wore a brown broadcloth coat, a scarlet damaskin lappel waistcoat, breeches over which his shirt hung, a black cordovan neckerchief decked with silver bugles, shoes and stockings and a hat. His ears were hung with pendants of brass and other wires plaited together like the handle of a basket."

Washington's Indian allies wanted to dress like Montour.

The colonel robbed his own wardrobe, extracting from it a shirt with ruffles to give to one Indian. Since he had but three shirts, he was unable to supply all the presents he would have liked to give, and so he sent expresses to Major Carlyle and the governor, imploring them to hurry with food and presents.

He received temporary relief when the first detachment of 100 men from South Carolina came down the road from Wills Creek with enough flour to last four days and 60 cattle. Their officer, Captain Mackay, also brought a peck of trouble. He had a commission from the king, and although he was only a captain, he claimed to outrank Washington. Not only that, he contended that his men, being real soldiers, serving under a captain with a king's commission, did not need to work. They lolled about, looking with disdain on the Virginians, who toiled like Negro slaves.

Washington complained to Dinwiddie that Mackay's attitude was wrecking morale. Dinwiddie attempted to resolve the difficulty by sending word that Colonel Innes of North Carolina was in chief command. He had fought in the War of Jenkins Ear and held a commission from the king that outdated and outranked that of Mackay. Second in rank he named Washington, third Captain Clark of New York, and fourth Captain Mackay.

The order did not faze Mackay. He recognized no authority of Virginia's governor over him. As for Innes, he was on the east side of the mountains. Until he arrived, Mackay would take no orders from a Virginia boy with nothing but a colonial commission. The two commands occupied adjoining camps and the commanders met and talked things over with neither admitting the authority of the other. Washington's men continued to make a road, working toward Gist's settlement.

Arrived at Gist's, Washington decided against proceeding to Redstone, still sixteen miles away. He sent all of his wagons but two back to Wills Creek to bring up provisions and to help Innes move. His men took shelter in the cabins of Gist's settlement, for the settlers had taken their families away from the scene of impending battle.

Now Indian scouts reported that the French with their Indian allies, 900 strong, had left Fort Duquesne in a move toward Washington's position. The commander called a council of war to consider their plight. Gist's settlement was indefensible, for it was surrounded with woods. The enemy could keep to the cover of trees and approach within a few feet of the English without being seen. Further, Half King threatened to leave if the command remained at Gist's settlement. While he and Aliquippa had but 25 warriors, they were invaluable as scouts. The council, therefore, decided to withdraw to the Great Meadows and there await Innes.

Since the army had only two wagons, they were insufficient to carry the supplies. Washington and other Virginia officers gave their horses to be packed with supplies while they walked. The men had to drag the nine cannon. When they reached the Great Meadows, the Indian scouts brought the news that the French had landed at Redstone and were moving toward Gist's. Thereupon, Half King and Aliquippa with their followers faded into the forest toward the east. They were not cowards, but neither were they intrepid. They saw no sense in fighting when it was no use.

That winter Tanacharison fell ill. He declared the French had put a hex on him, and he could not fight a hex. He grew worse and died of the malady.

Washington and Mackay together commanded 448 men. The count of the scouts said the French numbered 900. Innes had 800 North Carolinians, South Carolinians, Virginians, and New Yorkers. If he should join Washington, they would outnumber the French. Anxiously the English looked up Washington's road toward Wills Creek for signs of Innes. All that came was one wagon containing a cask of rum and a few bags of flour. Since the men had had no flour for several days, they feasted on bread, rolling it around on their tongues and enjoying it to the last taste.

Washington assigned Stobo to direct the completion of Fort Necessity. Never did a construction crew have greater incentive to work, for they were to erect a structure that would protect them from bullets, and yet the South Carolinians continued to loll in the shade. It was late in the afternoon of July 1 when the army came back to the Great Meadows. The weather was hot and the Virginians sweat as they toiled. It was still hotter the next day. The day dawned sultry, portending rain. Men worked as best they could, cursing the South Carolinians and their captain.

Every now and then a man would drop out. He could work no longer. The water of Meadows Run which supplied them had become contaminated. Dysentery spread through the camp. More than 100 Virginians were unfit for work.

By the night of July 2 the fort was as ready for defense as it ever would be. Its outer line was a parapet three logs high banked with earth. At nine points were emplacements for the cannon. Inside the parapet was a trench, in which men could stand while they fired over the top of the parapet or through loopholes. To economize on labor, Stobo utilized, where he could, natural ditches that had been cut in time of rain as water was drained from the Meadows into the run. At one corner of the parapet the men could get a drink.

In the center of the fort was a stockade 57 feet in diameter, loopholed for rifles and muskets. Within this citadel was a hut 14 feet square, roofed over with shakes, which offered protection to the more seriously ill and was a storehouse for powder. Now if Innes would only come with flour!

XII. *Villiers Vows Vengeance*

THE leader of the advancing Frenchmen was Captain Coulon de Villiers, within whose heart flamed outright hate for Washington. He was at Montreal when the tidings came of the Battle of Jumonville Glen and the death of Jumonville. "My brother must be avenged," he cried. With Abenakis, Nipissings, and Algonquin canoemen, he made a rapid voyage to Fort Duquesne, arriving just as the French, under arms, were ready to embark in canoes on the Monongahela. From Contrecoeur he begged permission to command so that he personally could defeat and humble Washington. Contrecoeur agreed and the flotilla set out, carrying 900 French and Indians.

At Redstone warehouse, Villiers told off a squad commanded by a sergeant to guard the canoes, while the main army started into the forest. A priest accompanied the army a few miles, then halted the men, permitting each man to confess his sins in his heart, absolving them and administering communion. Villiers sent Indian scouts to screen the advance and keep up a continuous line of information. In this way Villiers learned that Washington was planning to make a stand at Fort Necessity, that the fort was strong, but that the English had little food. Cattle grazed outside the palisade and could be run off. Villiers had only such food as his men could carry, but he felt that by making a swift attack, he could defeat Washington before Innes could come up.

The French advance was by way of Gist's settlement, which they found abandoned. Villiers paused in the road nearest to

Jumonville Glen. Then he went through the woods to the Glen where, in the presence of his brother's spirit, he vowed vengeance. He marched nearer to the Great Meadows and bivouacked the night of July 2.

During the night it rained, wetting the French and Indians. At Fort Necessity it wet the English as well. Indian scouts sent by Villiers observed Necessity during the night. One of them shot an English sentry in the heel. It threw the garrison into apprehension. To the English, every laurel clump, every chestnut stump was a foe. But after a time the camp quieted and the men bedded down again on the sodden ground. The rain fell heavier, drumming on the chestnut leaves.

As day broke the English killed a few beeves and had a breakfast of meat. Then they turned the cattle out to graze. For several hours they waited, looking back on Washington's road toward Wills Creek for Innes and looking forward toward Gist's for Villiers.

At eleven o'clock Washington saw the first signs of the French advancing in three columns. The Indians had put aside their blankets and came naked in the rain.

Washington and Mackay conferred and agreed to make a brave show by lining up all but the sick in front of the palisade. There they stood to show they were unafraid, as they were indeed, all but Muse, who remained inside the palisade. The French countered by drawing up in battlefront at a distance of 600 yards. The French gave a shout. The Indians raised a warwhoop and both French and Indians fired a volley, setting the songbirds awing. It was pure show. They knew their bullets would not carry effectively more than 100 yards.

The French and Indians now advanced, flanking the fort, keeping to the cover of trees and killing cattle. Here and there were lone trees and clumps of laurel on the Meadows. The

French and Indians darted from tree to tree, some getting to within 60 yards of the palisade. Washington and Mackay withdrew their men inside the palisade, stationing them in the trenches and warning them to shoot only after careful and deliberate aim. The battle continued through the afternoon and into the night. "The French," commented Washington, "'kept up a constant, galling fire from every rising, tree, stump, stone or bush."

The cannon, on which the English had relied, proved of no value. The French were so scattered it was more effective to use a rifle. Further, since the cannon barrels extended outside the palisade, it was necessary for the cannoneers to expose themselves so they could swab the guns and ram home a fresh charge at the muzzle.

The best ally of the French was the rain. Washington described it as a "most tremendous rain." Meadows Run could not carry it off. Water collected in the trenches, driving the men out. Since the trenches were immediately back of the palisades there was not room enough to lie in the mud between trenches and palisades. This deprived the English of their only shelter from enemy fire except for the stockade, which was not large enough to contain them all.

There was one encouragement. The South Carolinians, while disdaining labor, fought manfully. Both Virginians and Carolinians fired at will. They loaded their pieces, waited for an enemy to show his head, and then squeezed the trigger. Eventually, however, the rain soaked into the guns. When the enemy offered a target and a rifleman pulled a trigger, the flint sparked but the spark only hissed in the wet powder. When that happened, it was necessary to draw out the wet charge with a ramrod fitted with a screw.

Those back home who had failed to send food, and reinforcements and gifts for the Indians now failed again. There were but two screws in the entire army. Apparently the French and Indians had trouble, too, with fouled guns, but unfortunately for Washington, he did not know how badly off the French and Indians were. Their situation was summed up by Villiers in his written report, which stated: "As we had been wet all day by the rain, as the soldiers were very tired, as the savages said they would leave us the next morning, and as there was a report that drums and firing of cannon had been heard in the distance, I proposed to M. Le Mercier (the second in command) to offer the English a conference."

After dark Mercier called out, "Do you want to parley?" Washington refused, but a circumstance made him change his mind. After the coming of dark, some of the men had broken open the cask of rum. Soon large numbers were so drunk they were unfit for duty. Had the French risked a charge, they could have overrun the English.

When Mercier called a second time and proposed a parley, Washington and Mackay agreed. They sent Van Braam, who returned with written terms for the English capitulation. It included a surrender of the fort and the arms of all the men. Washington and Mackay rejected the proposal. To surrender their arms would put them at the mercy of the Indians.

Van Braam went back for a further parley. He was gone for an hour before he returned with the articles of capitulation. The new terms provided that the English could keep their arms and ammunition. They must surrender eight of their cannon and the fort. A small force should be left to care for the sick and wounded until wagons could be sent from Wills Creek. The English must agree not to advance into the Ohio for at least a year. In the text, Villiers inserted a word that would in some measure avenge his brother. He wrote that the French had no intention of disturbing the *bonne harmonie* between the kings of England and of France but to avenge the *assassinat* of a king's officer.

Since the articles were in French and since Van Braam was the translator, the English had to rely on him. He translated *assassinat* as death. Washington and Mackay saw no harm in that and let it go. Finally, the prisoners taken at Jumonville Glen were to be released. Since Washington did not have the prisoners and they were at Williamsburg, Villiers demanded that Washington must surrender two officers as hostages.

Stobo and Van Braam were willing to be hostages. Probably Stobo thought it would be an adventure to travel to the Ohio and visit the French fort. Van Braam, who was ready for any adventure, agreed, except that he did not have suitable clothing. He offered to buy Washington's broadcloth coat with silver fringes and his laced scarlet waistcoat. Washington gave the two garments to him and received in exchange from Van Braam an assignment of £16 of his wages.

The officers agreed to accept the articles of surrender. Washington signed first, but Mackay, claiming higher rank, signed above him. The next day was the fourth of July, but it was not a glorious day for Washington. When the rain that had defeated them ceased, each side buried its dead. Washington had lost 12 killed and 43 wounded. Mackay reported a loss of 18 killed and wounded. Villiers lost 20 killed and 52 wounded.

As the English were preparing to march out, French private soldiers began robbing them. One Frenchman seized a portmanteau belonging to Captain Adam Stephen. Stephen was wet and muddy. His face was powder burned and he wore no insignia of rank. He caught the Frenchman, kicked him, and recovered his portmanteau. French officers rallied a squad of men to punish Stephen, but he opened the portmanteau to reveal a gold laced uniform, thereby proclaiming his rank. The Frenchmen recognized the right of an officer to kick them, even a defeated enemy, and they let him alone.

As agreed with Villiers, the English marched out with drums beating and colors flying and dragging one cannon. They had gone only a short distance when the Indians came upon them and robbed some of the men. Among the Indians were Delawares, who recognized some of their Virginia acquaintances and shook hands with them.

The dejected troops made their way to Wills Creek, and, after sending wagons for their wounded, Washington and Mackay went on to Williamsburg. As though the defeat was not enough, they were to be humiliated still more a few months later when the Paris journals published the articles of surrender in which Washington admitted the assassination of Jumonville. British officers were highly critical. Washington, so they said, had advanced too far and had shown stupidity in signing the capitulation containing the word assassination.

In Virginia they blamed Van Braam for not translating correctly. Some even accused him of selling out to the French. This was unfair. Van Braam was not as good a linguist as he pretended. He simply did not know the difference between assassination and murder or death.

The House of Burgesses voted the thanks of Virginia to Washington and all of the officers except Van Braam and Muse. They excluded Van Braam because of his faulty translation, and Muse had showed cowardice. Governor Dinwiddie received Washington kindly. To his friend Colonel Innes he wrote: "The Misfortune attending our Expedit'n is entirely owing to the delay of your Forces, and more particularly to the two Ind't Compa's from N. Y.; how they can answer to their disobedience to His Majesty's Com'ds I know not."

XIII. *Washington Quits*

AS SOON as the English had departed from the Great Meadows, Villiers retired to Redstone, burned the Ohio Company warehouse there, and descended the Monongahela to Fort Duquesne. Since the transportation facilities of the French required rivers, they had no means of supplying a garrison at the Great Meadows. Contrecoeur, therefore, intended to rely on raiding parties of Indians accompanied by French officers to retain control of the territory back from the water courses.

Dinwiddie learned of what the French were doing and ordered Colonel Innes to prepare for a fall campaign against Duquesne. This was contrary to the articles of surrender Mackay and Washington had signed, which provided that the English "give their word of honor that they will work on no establishments either in the surrounding country or beyond the Highlands during one year from this day." It angered Washington when Dinwiddie explained that he was not bound by any surrender agreed to by a subordinate.

To Washington, the governor directed: "Get your regiment completed to 300 men. That there be no delay, I order you to march with what companies you have complete, and leave orders with the officers remaining to follow you, as soon as they shall have enlisted men sufficient to make up their companies. . . . I trust much to your dilligence and dispatch."

Washington raged to William Fairfax: "I have orders to complete my regiment, and not a sixpence is sent for that purpose. . . . There is not a man that has a blanket."

Dinwiddie was asking the impossible. To begin with Innes had no army. Even before the defeat at Necessity, a majority of the North Carolinians, not having been paid what had been promised and suffering from lack of food and clothing, had mutinied and straggled home afoot across Virginia, shoes broken, clothing ragged, begging for food from farmhouse to farmhouse. The New Yorkers, when they arrived in Virginia, had only one keg of powder and one half of it spoiled. Mackay's company, except for those killed, wounded, and sick, was still fit for service. As for the Virginians, even a rumor that another campaign was contemplated caused them to desert in groups. Six disappeared in a single night, and Washington commented: "This we expect, unless prevented by close confinement."

Dinwiddie further outraged Washington by ruling that the colonel had no authority to agree that the French prisoners taken at Jumonville Glen should be released, for the prisoners were held at Williamsburg and were not in Washington's possession. The governor particularly would not release La Force, because of his influence over the Indians.

This meant that Van Braam and Stobo, given as hostages as a guarantee for the return of the prisoners, must remain in prison at Duquesne. La Force escaped, but his English was so faulty, he was soon recaptured and locked up more securely. Stobo improved his time by drawing a plan of Fort Duquesne. This was easily done, for he had considerable liberty within the fort. He even went outside, conferred with an English-speaking Delaware there, and engaged him to carry the plans of the fort to Williamsburg for delivery to Dinwiddie. The governor paid the Indian and filed the plans for the future.

Dinwiddie took another step that would soon affect Washington. He called the governors of North Carolina and Maryland into conference and there offered to Governor Horatio

Sharpe of Maryland the command of all troops to be raised by the southern colonies. Sharpe, who had some slight military training, accepted. Dinwiddie thus effaced himself for the good of the cause. He knew he was no soldier himself and thought perhaps that Sharpe could do better. Further, he hoped this would cause Maryland to contribute men and money. In fact, the Maryland legislature responded by voting £6000 and two companies of men.

Sharpe ordered the building of a fort at Wills Creek, naming it Fort Cumberland in honor of the Duke of Cumberland, captain general of the British army and a son of the king.

Sharpe then issued an order that any officer with a king's commission, no matter how low, should outrank any colonial officer with a governor's commission, no matter how high. Further, no governor could issue a commission of higher rank than captain. Washington had an answer for that. He resigned. Dinwiddie was greatly displeased with the resignation. He felt that Washington was needed. Whether Dinwiddie appealed to Sharpe or not is uncertain. Anyway, Sharpe asked Washington to reconsider, offering him the title of colonel, but the pay and rank of a captain. To this Washington flung back: "If you think me capable of holding a commission, that has neither rank nor emolument annexed to it, you must entertain a very contemptible opinion of my weakness." He added: "I shall have the consolation of knowing that I have opened the way, when the smallness of our numbers exposed us to the attacks of a superior enemy; that I have hitherto stood the heat and brunt of the day."

Washington was out of a job a very short time. He owned 2000 acres of land. Since it was in scattered parcels and unimproved, he had leased it to adjoining planters. It was not immediately available for farming. But there was Mount Vernon. The will of Lawrence Washington provided that, if his daughter

Sarah survived, Mount Vernon should go to her. But Sarah died a few weeks after her father. In that event Lawrence's widow Anne should receive a life interest, after which it should go to George. Anne had nothing but tragic memories of Mount Vernon. She had borne four children there and had buried them there. There, too, she had buried her husband.

Five months after Lawrence's death, George Lee, a rich planter, offered to marry her. She agreed and moved to his plantation. Washington, thinking he had renounced the army forever, offered to take over Mount Vernon for Anne. She and her husband were willing. In November, 1754, she signed a lease to her life interest for 15,000 pounds of tobacco a year. The lease included the services of 18 slaves who belonged to the land. Mount Vernon, containing 2500 acres and wharves on the Potomac, came to Washington with a clear title when Anne died in 1761.

Washington later bought more land, expanding Mount Vernon to 9000 acres. Eventually he increased the plantation house from a story and a half to two and a half stories and added wings. In addition to Mount Vernon, Washington added to his land holdings by taking great acreages in what are now Pennsylvania and West Virginia. In time he became the richest landowner in America.

Washington was soon to discover that he was mistaken about ending his career as a soldier. The king's government in England, smarting under the humiliation of the defeat of Colonial troops at Fort Necessity, determined to wipe out the shame.

The government ordered Major General Edward Braddock to America with two regiments of 500 men each. He had spent 45 of his 60 years in the army and was rated a skillful and courageous officer. At the Battle of Culloden he had broken the enemy by his headlong charges, much to the satisfaction of the Duke of Cumberland, his commander looking on.

When Braddock set sail with Irish, Scotch, and English troops, the French ambassador at London demanded an explanation of the British prime minister, since England and France were at peace. The prime minister assured the ambassador that Braddock was on a peaceful mission. Thereupon France dispatched Baron Dieskau to Canada with 4000 men, assuring the British that this, too, was a mission of peace. Sailing with Dieskau was Marquis Pierre Francois Rigaud Vaudreuil to become governor of Canada. He was to replace Duquesne, who had resigned because of illness and age.

Braddock arrived in Virginia in February, 1755, and conferred with the colonial governors, who agreed with him on a four-pronged offensive. The northern colonies, having suffered from the ravages of intermittent war with the French and Indians of Canada since 1689, volunteered by the thousands when Governor William Shirley of Massachusetts told them this would be a war to end all wars in America.

The first prong of the offensive was a move by sea to Nova Scotia, home of the Acadians, who offered no resistance. The English took the Acadians from their homes and scattered them through the English colonies. Second, Shirley was to lead a column to take Fort Niagara. This would cut off supplies from Canada to Fort Duquesne and stop the fur trade between Canada and the Great Lakes. The third column, to be led by William Johnson, was to take Crown Point on Lake Champlain.

Braddock would lead the fourth column. He would capture Fort Duquesne, march north, take Venango, Fort Le Boeuf, and Presque Isle, then join Shirley. The two would combine with Johnson and the three columns would converge on Quebec to destroy New France.

The plan had elements of hope for success. The English colonial population was about 1,000,000. New France, including Canada, Louisiana, and the undefined region between, numbered one tenth that figure. Johnson and Shirley had limited military experience, but Shirley was a lawyer and a student of Roman history. He had read Caesar's accounts of his campaigns in the original Latin and fancied himself a soldier. Johnson's wife was a Mohawk. He was owner of a great estate on the Mohawk River, where he enjoyed the friendship of the Iroquois Indians and could count on them to fight on his side.

An English weakness was a lack of co-operation between the colonies and within the colonies. Each colony was independent of the other. Further the legislatures, which were elected by the people, often were at variance with the governors most of whom were appointed by the crown. By contrast, the voice of the governor of Canada was obeyed from the seas that washed Gaspe to the far prairies beyond Lac Que Parle.

It is true that Braddock was commander-in-chief, but his authority extended only to the armed forces. Representatives of five colonies met at Albany to work out a plan of unity, but that was all the Albany Congress could do. It was still up to the legislatures to vote men and money. The greatest unifying force was the prestige of Braddock in whom all reposed the highest confidence. Of him Dinwiddie commented: "He is a very fine officer, and a sensible, considerate gentleman. He and I live in great harmony."

Enthusiasm caused the Virginia Burgesses to vote £40,000 to pay and equip 450 Virginians in nine companies. Washington must have reflected that with half that much he could have given presents to the Indians and enrolled men enough to give him victory at Fort Necessity. In addition about 400 more Virginians volunteered to serve in Braddock's two regiments, thereby bringing that force up to 1400 men.

Montour and Croghan enrolled 80 Indian warriors, who brought 120 wives and children to Fort Cumberland. Braddock also was enrolling volunteers from North Carolina, South Carolina, and Maryland. From all this warlike preparation Washington held himself aloof. He was planning to seed his fields. Among other things he had to produce 15,000 pounds of tobacco for Anne or lose his lease on Mount Vernon. He had cause for worry, for the season was dry. Some weeks later his mother was to write him that on account of lack of rain, the pastures were so dry that the cows were producing insufficient milk to churn butter.

Then came a letter from Braddock, asking Washington to meet him at Alexandria, only a dozen miles from Mount Vernon. Braddock was holding a conference of governors there. Of course Farmer Washington was pleased with the recognition. Of course he had a slave saddle a horse. Of course he put on his best suit and rode away to the north.

XIV. *The Shades of Death*

IT IS probable that Dinwiddie told Braddock that Washington had a will to fight and could be of value, but that he would not serve under king's officers of lower rank than his own. Braddock had a plan. When Washington arrived, the general offered him a place on his staff as an aide. He would have no rank to bother him, no men to command, and no men who would command him, except the general who would give orders that Washington would transmit to others. Perhaps he flattered the farmer by saying he needed the advantage of Washington's experience in the region beyond the Narrows.

Washington was introduced to the governors. Shirley paid considerable attention to the Virginian. His 60-year-old blood must have tingled at the sight of the youthful farmer. If Washington, with a forlorn command of undisciplined recruits, could accomplish so much, why could not Shirley, with his knowledge of Caesar's campaigns, do better as he marched to Niagara with an adequate force back of him? To William Fairfax, Washington related: "I have the honor to be introduced to several governors and of being well received by Mr. Shirley, whose character and appearance have perfectly charmed me."

Washington also met William Shirley, Jr., son of the governor, who was learning the art of war while serving as Braddock's secretary. Young Shirley was to suffer disappointment. He found he was not learning under Braddock and wrote a critical letter about his general. He found Braddock's subordinates unsatisfactory, too, as he said: "Some are ignorant and insolent, others capable, but rather aiming at showing their own abilities."

But for the moment the young secretary was full of enthusiasm and energy. He infected Washington with his military ardor so much that the Virginian decided to accept the general's offer. Riding to Fredericksburg, he asked his 19-year-old brother Jack to come over from his mother's farm and take charge of Mount Vernon. William Fairfax, master of Belvoir, agreed to serve as Jack's adviser while George was helping to whip the French. Nobody dreamed that Braddock might fail.

Assured that his farm would be in good hands, Washington rode to Fort Cumberland, where an army of 2400 men was assembling. This included volunteers from Pennsylvania, Maryland, and the Carolinas and 300 axmen, skilled in the use of both the musket and ax, who would complete Washington's road from Gist's settlement to Fort Duquesne.

Also assembled were 600 horses, including pack animals and wagon teams. Many of the horses, however, were spavined, broken hocked, and wind galled, which caused Washington to lament: "There has been vile management in horses."

Braddock fumed over the contractors who were more concerned with making a fast doubloon than with providing sound horses and wagons. Benjamin Franklin, learning of the bad situation, voluntarily and without a cent of profit, obtained 150 good Pennsylvania wagons and teams, giving his personal word that they would be paid for by the British army. Braddock was so pleased with Franklin that he wrote: "This he accomplished with promptitude and fidelity, and is almost the only instance of address and integrity, which I have seen in these provinces."

Washington and Braddock liked each other from the first. The Virginian was Mr. Washington with no rank, although he was called colonel by courtesy. He was a volunteeer, serving without pay, supplying his own uniform and riding his own horses from Mount Vernon. He studied Braddock's military organization, learning what he could from that noted commander. No longer was he learning the art of war by trial and error. Now, so he thought, he was learning at the elbow of a master.

Besides Braddock, Washington found excellent company. Young Shirley, while critical of Braddock's subordinates, made an exception of Washington. Captain Roger Morris and Captain Robert Orme, also aides to Braddock, were friendly. One of Braddock's colonels, Sir Peter Halkett, had brought with him his two sons, James and Francis, subalterns in the army, who had heard of Washington and were interested in the frontiersman who never bragged or intruded but could answer questions about the Ohio because he had been there.

At no time did Washington offer advice to Braddock unless the general asked for it. Then he replied, giving facts clearly as one convinced that he knew what he was talking about. By bitter experience Washington would learn later that the perfect drill of the British regulars was a handicap in bushwhacker warfare, but at the present he was filled with admiration.

His appreciation was nothing to the awe the regulars inspired in the Indians. The French sent Indian scouts from Fort Duquesne to reconnoiter. From boulders or trees or screens of rhododendron thickets the scouts, with mouths agape, watched the regulars in fascination. An entire regiment maneuvered as one man in perfect cadence, every foot in exact step, every hand swinging in unison, every burnished button reflecting the sun, every polished saber and bayonet gleaming like silver, and every British coat scarlet as blood.

They had admiration for the officers, booted to the knees

and weighted with gold braid. They agreed that Braddock was most resplendent. Around his middle he wound a pure white sash, big enough to make a hammock. By contrast, the Virginians, such as had uniforms of blue, were drab. Those in homespun were even more drab. Braddock contemptuously asserted: "Their slothful and languid disposition renders them unfit for military service."

The British officers were shocked at what they called the insolence of the Americans. For example, there was 19-year-old Daniel Morgan, whiplash champion, who was driving his own team and wagon for hire. When rebuked by an officer for being late, he countered with a rough retort, just as he would sass back a fellow Virginian. Out swished the officer's sword as he rushed toward Morgan. The wagoner caught the blade with the cracker of his blacksnake whip, dashing it out of the officer's hand to the ground.

The officer, cursing threats, dismounted to retrieve it, and Morgan, leaping from his wagon, thrashed him. British soldiers tied Morgan by the wrists to the tailgate of his wagon and started to administer 500 lashes on the bare back. Every lash raised a livid welt until 450 had been dealt. Even Morgan could take no more and fell unconscious. They threw water on him to restore him, and he again mounted his wagon seat and drove. Such brutality horrified Croghan's Indians, who reserved torture for their enemies.

As for Morgan, he nurtured his hatred for 20 years. When the War for Independence began, he raised a company and fought with such zeal and purpose that he was promoted again and again, attaining the rank of general. He was the same General Morgan that fought so effectively at the Battle of Saratoga as to turn the tide and force the surrender of the British Burgoyne.

Among the witnesses to the whiplashing was a fellow wagoner, 20-year-old Daniel Boone of North Carolina, later the foremost Kentucky frontiersman, who, after he had married and had a family, named one of his boys Daniel Morgan in honor of the man who parried a whip against a naked sword.

Braddock abhorred Morgan's lack of respect for a British officer, but he was flabbergasted one day when a squad of men from Pennsylvania's Juniata forest slouched to his tent, led by Captain Jack, also called Black Hunter and Black Rifle. He told Braddock how one evening, upon returning from a hunting trip, he found his cabin in smoldering embers amid which lay his wife and children, scalped and otherwise mutilated. He rallied a band of taciturn frontiersmen, who vowed no-quarter vengeance and had come, he said, to serve Braddock as scouts. They asked for permission to range the forest ahead of the army, live on wild game and scout, kill and scalp, all without pay. They reserved only that while in camp they were to enjoy freedom from camp chores and discipline.

Braddock studied their faces painted like Indians and smeared with grease to repel mosquitoes. He glanced at their moccasins and breech clouts. Churlishly he directed that they scrub off their grease. Turning their backs and without a word, they slouched into the forest, and Braddock failed to realize that he was losing a force that might measure the difference between triumph and death.

The general, after consulting with Washington, Gist, and Croghan, made much over the Indians. He provided all the beef they could gorge into their mouths. He gave them flour and rum and desirable presents. Reciprocating what they thought was his affection, the redmen intruded on Braddock's presence so consistently that he became peevish. He was troubled, too, by his own British soldiers, who visited the women in the Indian camp. They were especially fond of a vivacious siren, Bright Lightning. When Braddock had the men lashed for frequenting the women's tepees, and they persisted in their offense, he ordered all Indian families to withdraw. Most of the warriors, resentful, followed Captain Jack's trail into the woods, and once more the general had no sense of loss. He still had eight Mingoes, who remained loyal to the British, along with Croghan, Montour, and Gist. He thought he had enough.

Upon arrival at Gist's settlement, Braddock resolved not to march to the Monongahela at Redstone. Instead he moved north, crossed the Youghiogheny, spent one night at Captain Jacobs cabins, and moved toward Turtle Creek.

Braddock has been accused of taking no precautions against ambuscade. This is not entirely correct. He did the best he knew how and often consulted with Washington, Croghan, and Gist on the matter. His advance was headed each day by a guard of highly trained British riflemen. Ahead of them rode six blue-clad Virginians, selected for their knowledge of the woods. On the flanks he kept outriders, constantly alert for an enemy. Behind the advance guard moved 300 axmen, extending Washington's road beyond Gist's. It was now Braddock's Road, 12 feet wide so that wagons could pass going in either direction. According to Washington his army was strung out over too long a line of march. Since Braddock did not ask his advice on the matter, Washington followed his usual practice and offered none. He did, however, write his brother Jack: "They had often a line three or four miles in length; and the soldiers guarding [the wagons] were so dispersed, that if we had been attacked either in front, center, or rear, the part so attacked must have been cut off, or totally routed, before they could be sustained by any other corps."

At about this time an express rider, belaboring his exhausted horse, came up with a message from William Johnson. His Mohawk scouts had seen 300 of Dieskau's French regulars in boats on Lake Ontario, apparently going to reinforce Contrecoeur at Fort Duquesne. The general consulted Washington, who wrote to Jack: "I urged him to push forward, if he did it with a small but chosen band. . . . I urged that if we could credit our intelligence, the French were weak at the Fork at present, but hourly expecting reinforcements, who, to my certain knowledge, could not arrive with provisions, or any supplies, during the continuance of the drouth."

There were added reasons for haste. Since passing the Great Meadows, the horses had eaten little grass. Corn was in short supply since it had to be hauled in the wagons. The horses browsed on twigs, which, no matter how nourishing to the wood buffalo, were not a sustaining feed for horses. Teams weakened until they were unfit to be hitched.

Dysentery, the old enemy of the soldier, appeared next. Washington was among those incapacitated. For three weeks in late June and early July he was confined to a bed beside the trail or in a wagon.

There was yet a final reason for haste. The British soldiers, unaccustomed to an interminable forest, were growing timorous. They spoke of the gloomy woods as the shades of death. They imagined hostile eyes peering from every laurel bush or smilax vine. Indian scouts from Fort Duquesne stimulated their apprehension by firing unexpectedly on the column, and outriders who charged into the timber found nothing but moccasin tracks. But, let a man straggle from the column and he lost his scalp.

To be killed was bad. Sometimes it was worse to be captured. There was 20-year-old James Smith, who enlisted as an axman, hoping to earn wages so he could come home with British coin in his pockets and marry his girl. He was captured and taken to Fort Duquesne. As his captors were approaching the fort, they screeched the gauntlet whoop. Several hundred

Jay-Bee Photo

Looking east into Pittsburgh. The Allegheny River coming from the left and the Monongahela from the right form the Ohio in the foreground.

Washington's office in Winchester, Virginia, as it appears today.

Courtesy Ross E. Mohney. Winchester Chamber of Commerce

Palace of the Governors in
Williamsburg, restored to appear
as it was when Governor
Dinwiddie lived there.

Robert Dinwiddie, from a
painting by an unidentified
artist in the National Portrait
Gallery, London.

Thomas, Lord Fairfax, from a painting by Jacobus Houbraken. Engraving from collection of Colonial Williamsburg.

Lawrence Washington, from a painting hung in the library at Mt. Vernon by George Washington. Mt. Vernon Ladies Association.

The Narrows. The way through the mountains west of Cumberland. Air photo, courtesy Anthony Laeli, Cumberland Chamber of Commerce.

Fort Necessity, as restored in 1954.

Benjamin Franklin in 1759. Painting by Benjamin Wilson, White House Collection, Washington.

General Edward Braddock

Daniel Lienard de Beaujeu, taken from a bracelet miniature he gave to his wife. *Pennsylvania Magazine of History and Biography.*

Governor William Shirley, by T. Hudson. Engraving by J. McArdell.

Sir William Johnson, by John Woolaston, the younger. Albany Institute and Historical and Art Society Collection.

Marquis de Montcalm. Collection of La Corne de Saint Luc and Jacques Viger. Given to University of Laval by Abbe H-D Verreau, 1901.

Colonel John Armstrong, by
Rembrandt Peale. Collection of
Independence Hall, National
Historical Park.

Robert Rogers, from a 1777
German print, republished in
Ponteach, Caxton Club, Chi-
cago, 1914.

Colonel William Byrd III, by Cosmo
Alexander, in the Virginia State Library,
Richmond.

Martha Custis, by John Woolaston, a year before her marriage to George Washington. Collection of Washington and Lee University.

John Parke and Martha Custis, children of Mrs. Martha Washington, by John Woolaston. Collection of Washington and Lee University.

Colonel Henry Bouquet. Collection of the Historical Society of Pennsylvania.

George Washington at 40, in colonel's uniform worn in French and Indian War. By Charles Wilson Peal. Collection of Washington and Lee University.

John Robinson, member of House of Burgesses, by John Woolaston. Collection of Colonial Williamsburg.

General John Forbes, from an original in possession of the Royal Scots Greys Regiment, Aldershot, England. Western Pennsylvania Historical Society, Pittsburgh.

warriors spurted from their wigwams with clubs and formed in two lines. An English-speaking Delaware informed Smith that if he could run between the two lines and reach the fort alive, he would be spared. Like a swivel-hipped football half back, he dodged 300 blows and was almost at the stockade outside the fort when a well-aimed stroke felled him. As he tried to rise, an Indian threw sand in his eyes. Unable to see to dodge further, he was clubbed into insensibility.

When he recovered consciousness, Smith found himself inside the fort wondering why his life had been spared. After a few days he was visited by the English-speaking Delaware, who boasted regarding the advancing Braddock: "We'll shoot um down all one pigeon."

The snatching away of men like Smith conjured up visions of bugaboos and hobgoblins in the minds of the Britishers. Braddock knew it was important to get the campaign over. He presented Washington's plan for dividing the army at a war council without saying Washington had proposed it. The officers realized that to divide a force in the presence of an enemy is to move into the shadow of risk, but they all agreed it would be better to strike the enemy before Dieskau's forces arrived.

Braddock left his worst horses and wagons with Colonel Thomas Dunbar, who also was given the worst dressed men and the least reliable regulars. Dunbar was to follow as best he could. Braddock advanced with 30 wagons, some of the best cannon, a picked regiment of regulars commanded by Colonel Sir Peter Halkett and continued northward, intending to cross Turtle Creek, gain the high land above Fort Duquesne, and then coast down the ramp of land to the fort, attacking it from the heights.

He had learned from Croghan, Montour, Gist, and the Mingoes the full details of the terrain. From Dinwiddie, he had obtained Stobo's carefully drawn outline of the fort itself. Gist and two Mingoes, on a scouting expedition, returned with more details. Gist reported that he had reached the bluff just south of the Forks of the Ohio, from which he looked down into the fort itself. A cannon could be mounted there and shoot across the Monongahela into the stockade. He told Braddock that the French had not more than 250 white French and Canadians. The main garrison consisted of Indians, camped outside the stockade in huts.

The morning of July 9 found Braddock on the south bank of Turtle Creek, which flows into the Monongahela where Frazier's fort stood. Its banks were so precipitous the engineers estimated that it would take a full day to grade a crossing passable for wagons.

The scouts recommended a better plan. They would bypass the creek by marching to the Monongahela. Because of the drouth the river was easily fordable. Its rocky bed would support wagons and cannon. Acting on their advice, Braddock decided to cross the Monongahela, march past the mouth of Turtle Creek, and then cross back to be on the same side of the river as Fort Duquesne.

He directed Lieutenant Colonel Thomas Gage to rouse his guard of 300 men at 3 o'clock in the morning and seize the two crossings. Major Sir John St. Clair was to follow with 200 axmen, cutting a road. Gage was the same officer who sent British troops to Lexington and Concord in 1775, thereby starting the Revolutionary War. The seizure of the fords was easily accomplished. Indians from Fort Duquesne withdrew without even a token resistance.

At the first crossing of the Monongahela, Washington, who was riding on a bed in a wagon, ordered one of his horses brought up and saddled and had a pillow placed on the saddle. The fever had left him, but he was still weak from 20 days of illness. Across the river he saw Frazier's abandoned fort, where he and Gist had taken shelter 18 months before. Gone were the snow and ice. The trees that had been bleak when he had passed that way on his return from Le Boeuf were now verdant with foliage.

Washington rode forward to watch the soldiers at the second crossing. He later described what he saw as one of the most beautiful sights he had ever witnessed. The red-coated regulars splashed into the stream. The cool water was welcome on that clear July day, for the British uniforms were designed for wear in relatively cool England, Ireland, or Flanders. The river was so low that it exposed a pebbly beach a quarter of a mile wide. Here Braddock paraded his army with unfurled guidons and with drums beating and trumpets blaring. This was showmanship designed to awe the unseen Indians in the thickets.

It was now a little after noon. Braddock directed Gage to advance up the slope as fast as St. Clair's axmen could follow and hew a road. He was to proceed until 3 o'clock and then find a suitable place to camp. As Gage ascended the slope from the river, he came to a second bottom covered by a grove of stately walnut trees free of underbrush. It would have made a very good camping place, because visibility was good and approaching Indians would be more readily seen. But it was not yet 3 o'clock and so Gage continued his advance.

As he came to the slope above the second bottom, he found much underbrush, which annoyed him, but he had marched through underbrush before without serious trouble. He selected the most nearly clear place he could find, but to his right and left were continuous thickets of plum brush and above both thickets depending from the tree branches were festoons of grape vines. If Gage's outriders had penetrated the brush, they would have found that both the thickets concealed gullies from four to six feet deep and running parallel to the advance of the column. Beyond the gulley on his right, Gage could see a steep bluff rising abruptly from the gully. He scrutinized it as he looked over his right shoulder but under the mantle of trees he could see nothing moving. He was not particularly alarmed and continued to follow the six blue-coated Virginian vedettes, who reached a place 250 yards up the slope where more plum brush was in front of them, stretching across their course.

A bronze plaque marks the point where the vedettes arrived at the brush in front of them. It is situated about seven miles from the Forks of the Ohio in the steel-mill suburb of Braddock, which adjoins Pittsburgh on the southeast. The plaque is about a quarter of a block from a railroad overpass across which thunder trains with their cargoes of iron ore and fabricated steel. Nearby the stacks of a steel mill emit fumes to befoul the air. Between the plaque and the mill are millworkers homes, built solidly side to side close to the walks without any yards, and the children play in the streets.

It is hard today to conjure up the venerable forest that the vedettes rode through on that hot July day. You can look in vain for the flushed axmen, who 200 years ago toiled to cut away while sweat welled down their backs and flanks into their shoes. Even the vedettes, keen eyed though they were, caught only the faintest glimpses of wild beasts and missed entirely the naked warriors, skulking from tree to tree and thicket to thicket, retreating from the exotic notes of the band that rang through the woods that theretofore had known only the voice of nature and nature's creatures.

XV. *The Battle of the Monongahela*

THROUGH the weeks of Braddock's steady advance, Contrecoeur was shillyshallying at Fort Duquesne, unable to make up his mind. His heart told him to attack the English, but his head told him he had no chance. His position was unenviable.

A year before, after the beating of Washington at Fort Necessity, Governor Vaudreuil, thinking that the French position on the Ohio was secure, robbed Contrecoeur of most of his white soldiers, calling them to the defense of Canada against threats from Massachusetts and New York. Not until it was definitely known that Braddock intended to attack Fort Duquesne, did Vaudreuil detach 300 regulars from Dieskau's army to reinforce Contrecoeur and these reinforcements had not had time to arrive.

As Contrecoeur toured his camp he saw the most heterogeneous army ever assembled on this continent. There were Abenakis from Maine, Algonquins from the St. Lawrence, and Delawares, Shawnees, Wyandottes, and Mingoes from the Ohio. He had Braddock to thank for the Mingoes, who drifted into the French camp after the British general had alienated them. There were Miamis from the Miami, Ottawas from Detroit led by their own Pontiac, more Ottawas from Green Bay led by Charles Langlade, the destroyer of Pickawillany, who also led Ojibways, Chippewas, and Potawatomies from the pinelands and wild rice swamps of Wisconsin.

Captain Francis Ligneris brought Kickapoos, Mascoutins, and western Miamis, and from the banks of the Mississippi came Kaskaskias and Illinois. A band of Pawhuska's Osages came from as far as what is now Missouri and Otoes from what is now Nebraska. The Osages and Otoes came riding fleet-footed mustangs they had caught running wild on the western prairies, and looked down haughtily upon forest Indians crouched in canoes or plodding afoot. More horseback Indians were on the way, among them Kaws from Kansas who arrived too late to help.

Between the Osages and Abenakis there was a wider difference in language than between Russian and English. Even tribes living side by side, as the Wyandottes and Shawnees, took pride in their inability to understand each other. When Contrecoeur held a war council, he had to speak by signs or call a battery of interpreters.

The French commander was about to set Fort Duquesne afire and retreat to Venango, when an ensign, Chevalier de la Perade, returned from observing Braddock. From the concealment of various thickets he had watched the British in maneuvers and was greatly impressed with the manner in which they executed intricate evolutions in response to the general's command or to a note of a bugle. Of those who sat in the council hearing Perade's report only 44-year-old Captain Daniel Lienard de Beaujeu saw a flaw in British perfection. This captain had spent his adult life in the service of France. He had commanded at Niagara and Detroit and had dealt with Indians so much, he had become a master in understanding Indian mental processes. A native of Montreal, he had married a girl he had known from childhood, and he wished to win over Braddock so that he could return to his wife and family. Beaujeu declared that Braddock's troops were too well disciplined. They had been trained to do no thinking for themselves but to rely wholly on their commander, whom they obeyed with precision. Captain Jean Daniel Dumas agreed with Beaujeu.

The two spoke so confidently of victory that Contrecoeur gave Beaujeu permission to attempt an attack. He directed the French and Canadian soldiers to get ready to march, and authorized Beaujeu to call the Indians into council.

The night of July 8 already was darkening when the Indians assembled to hear Beaujeu. Speaking in French, which was translated by barking interpreters, Beaujeu explained that they had not attacked the English before because they lacked horses and wagons for hauling supplies. He was sure they could win. He suggested that each man supply himself with jerked beef and parched corn, and they would march that night to be near the enemy. The next morning as the English were entangled in the crossing of Turtle Creek or when the army was cut in two at a ford of the Monongahela, they would attack and destroy the advanced half before the rear half could cross over. He told of scalps to be taken, of stores to be gathered from the wagons, of red coats and gilt braid they could strip from the soldiers they would kill, and of the horses they could mount and ride like Pawhuska's Osages. In rebuttal a warrior, who because of the heat had come naked to the council fire, cried out: "What, father, do you wish to die and sacrifice us besides? They are 4000, we but 800. See, you have no sense."*

Other Indians cried agreement and started back for their huts. Only a few told Beaujeu they would have to think it over and would tell him in the morning. The failure of the council wrecked the opportunity to attack the English when they would be divided at the crossing of the Monongahela. Beaujeu, however, sent out Indians to observe the enemy and keep him advised by runners.

The next morning James Smith, the prisoner, still lame

* Quotations from the debate between Beaujeu and an unidentified Indian are from French reports as translated by John Gilmary Shea in Pennsylvania Magazine of History and Biography, Vol. VIII, June, 1884, Philadelphia.

from the beating he had received when he ran the gauntlet, hobbled with a stick to the catwalk near the top of the stockade where he could look down on the other side. He observed Beaujeu coming from the little log Chapel of the Assumption of the Blessed Virgin at the Beautiful River, where he had gone to confess his sins and receive the sacrament from the chaplain. Other French and Canadians followed his example, for on the morning of battle, who knows who will come back?

After breakfast the white soldiers assembled fully armed in front of the fort, and the naked Indians came to look on. Turning to them Beaujeu said: "I am determined to go and meet the enemy. I am sure to beat them. Will you let your father go alone?"

Some of the Indians understood and translated for the others. A chief ran to the gate of the fort where stood a barrel of powder with its head knocked open. He scooped up a small handful of powder, wet it, and blackened his face with it. To his mouth he put his hand and quavered a warwhoop. He filled his powder horn from the barrel and his bullet pouch from a keg. Then he ran to Beaujeu's side. Smith, from his battlement, saw the other warriors crowd about the barrel, shouting and getting powder and ball. Other Indians ran to their huts to paint their faces, for the proper painting brought luck.

Sometime between 8 and 9 o'clock Smith saw them make off like a rabble, the French and Canadians grouped around their officers, and the Indians, 637 of them, following their chiefs. With 72 French regulars and 146 Canadians, the force totaled 855, with which Beaujeu intended to meet 1451 Englishmen who had crossed the Monongahela. The Indians wore only breechclouts and moccasins. The French regulars wore uniforms. The Canadians were in shirts with their tails out over deerskin breeches. Beaujeu wore a hat and fringed buckskins. A silver gorget at his throat designated his rank.

After they had gone part way, some of the Indians refused to proceed further. Beaujeu had to call another council, and more precious time was lost. He taunted the Indians with having come so far to fight, and now that a fight was in the making, they wanted to run. By such methods did he persuade his allies to resume the march.

Having missed an opportunity to attack at the river crossing, Beaujeu kept watching for another favorable place to give battle. Apparently he kept scouts running to and fro to advise him of the position of the English. Suddenly a scout came running to say that the English had moved into a cul de sac, with thickets on three sides. Beaujeu had been over the ground

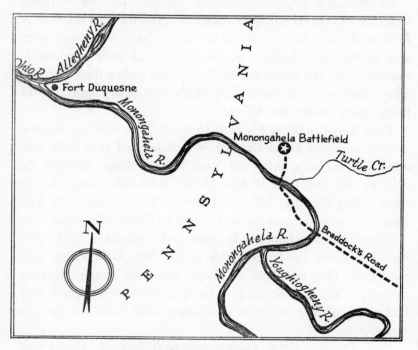

Monongahela battlefield

and knew the place. On the instant he improvised a plan of battle. Bounding forward he broke through the leafage to view the enemy for himself.

As he saw them advancing up the slope between the gullies fully screened by thickets, he jerked off his hat and swung it to the right and left, apparently directing the Indians to enter the gullies on either side. The French and Canadians, probably by prearrangement, held the center. The swinging of the hat was the only general order given by the French in the entire engagement. Officers and chiefs advised the men near them, but for the most part each man loaded and fired whenever he saw a good target. It was to be a battle of undisciplined warriors against meticulously trained troops.

As Beaujeu appeared he was spotted by the Virginia vedettes, who cried the alert. Gage ordered his men into battle front and gave the command to aim. There was nothing to aim at, but the obedient Britishers pointed their muskets at the brush. At the command of "fire," they pulled their triggers. The volley tore off leaves and twigs like heavy hail. Smoke hung heavy under the foliage.

Then Gage ordered his men to load. This took an interval as men rammed home charges of powder and then balls and adjusted the flints. After all were loaded, Gage ordered the men to aim and then to fire. Volley followed volley. At the third volley Beaujeu fell — a bullet in his forehead. By that time cannon had come up and added to the terrific noise.

More than one-half the Indians and Canadians broke and ran. Some fled the seven miles to the fort. Others ran until they knew they were out of range, and then paused to listen and see. They had decided to be spectators. They knew they had plenty of time to scatter and hide should Braddock become victorious.

With Beaujeu dead, Dumas was next in rank. He as well

as his other officers and the remaining Indian chiefs were quick to see that the British method of firing by volley left an interval in which the French and Indians could expose themselves and fire without danger of being shot at. When Gage cried "aim" there was still time to duck behind trees or into a gully. Since there had been no rain, the gullies, unlike the ditches at Fort Necessity the year before, were dry as dust.

Perade was killed soon after Beaujeu, but others fought on. Ligneris, Langlade, Pontiac, and Pawhuska ran down the gullies, their warriors following until they came to a spot where they might shoot at Englishmen. Some of the warriors who had fled at the onset of battle, now regained their courage and came back. They climbed the bluff on the British right to find vantage points from which to fire on the English below them.

Braddock could have withdrawn to the walnut grove and fought with better visibility, but to him retreat was a sign of weakness. He could have ordered his men to find cover behind trees. To the amazement of the Indians, he did not. Galloping up from the center, he ordered Lieutenant Colonel Burton, commanding at that point, to bring his troops to support Gage. With Braddock rode his secretary, Shirley, and his three aides, Orme, Morris, and Washington.

At the front he found the Virginia vedettes and flanking troops had taken to trees. The Pennsylvania axmen, having tossed aside axes and taken guns, were doing the same thing. Some of Gage's men were following their example. This act of simple prudence shocked him. In his 45 years of warfare he had never seen it done. With the flat of his sword he beat his own men away from the trees and sent his aides to order the Virginians to fight in the open. He directed various captains to lead charges into the brush. As they did so, the Indians scurried away, only to return after they had turned the charge into a rout by fire from the sides.

"It was like sending a cow to catch a rabbit," observed Adam Stephen.

Gage's officers, on horseback, were killed or wounded one by one. Gage himself was hit, but was able to remain in the saddle. His men fell back, mingling with St. Clair's axmen and Burton's regulars. This threw the ranks into confusion, for, fighting as they were in formation, they needed space to maneuver.

Captain Thomas Waggoner, who had been wounded at Jumonville Glen and later fought at Necessity, knew exactly what to do. Violating orders, he advanced with his company of 50 Virginians into the thicket where he directed them to use a fallen tree as a breastwork. Braddock could not see them there, and they were fighting effectively and driving out the enemy from that sector. Forty additional Virginians, whose captain had been killed, followed Waggoner and fought effectively beside him.

A British captain, bringing up his company to the front, noticed the irregular firing and thinking they were French, directed his company to fire a volley at the puffs of smoke. They fired a second and a third volley before Waggoner came back to join the British. Of 90 men who had gone to the shelter of that tree, only 30 came out unhit. The rest were killed or wounded, which is more than the French and Indians lost in the entire day.

Shirley was killed at Braddock's side. Orme and Morris were carried to the rear wounded. Washington, who had refrained from offering advice unless it was sought, now thought the emergency required him to speak. He proposed to Braddock that he let the Virginians seek shelter. Braddock could not unlearn 45 years of training. Let the French play the coward, his men must fight without seeking shelter. And so they continued to stand up helplessly. To fight them was as easy as shooting cows in a lot.

It is remarkable that the English lasted as long as they did. The first volley was fired at about two-thirty o'clock. They remained on the field more than three hours. Gage's men, having borne the brunt of the battle, having lost most of their officers, having been fired on by an enemy they could not see, did a human thing. They ran. They ran through Burton's battalion, ran past Halkett's men who were guarding the wagons and bringing up the rear, ran to the river and waded across. Gage rode after them, pleading that they rally and make a stand. In an effort to restore courage, Burton led his men in a charge, but was shot from his horse and carried on a litter to the rear. His men skedaddled. "They ran as sheep pursued by dogs," commented Washington.

A marvel of the day was Washington. Having risen from a sickbed in a wagon only that morning, weak and wan, he rode his horse by sheer will. After Shirley was killed and Orme and Morris wounded, he remained the general's only aide. He was everywhere, carrying Braddock's commands to this officer and that one. Since he rode tall in the saddle, he was a conspicuous mark amid the screaming bullets. The same guardian who had protected him when fired on while returning from Le Boeuf, who had spared him at Jumonville Glen and at Necessity, must have been hovering near again.

A Mingo chief bore witness to this. He recognized Washington as the same man who had carried the message to Le Boeuf a year and a half before and directed his warriors to bring him down. The chief, one of the best marksmen of his tribe, thought he had hit him. Four bullets left burns where they cut Washington's coat. Two horses they shot from under him, but each time he cleared the tumbling horse, mounted a second and a third and rode and rode. After the war was over the Mingo met Washington and told him that after they had shot in vain, the chief advised his men: "Aim at somebody you can kill. I am convinced that Washington is under the protection of the Great Spirit."

Having demoralized the front and center of the English army, the Indians attacked Halkett's regiment in the rear. The colonel was among the first to fall. His son James ran to help him and bent over him. A well-aimed bullet struck him and he fell dead across the body of his dead father.

The wagoners fought from the wagons but the Indians and French came at them from both flanks. Daniel Morgan, whose 450 lashes had left scars and scabs, was shooting in one direction when a bullet came from the other, struck him in the back of the neck and lodged in his mouth. He spat it out and kept firing.

With Halkett dead and the Indians crowding the wagons, and with British troops running by in terror, the drivers cut loose their loads, mounted their horses and galloped from the field bareback.

Shortly after 5:30 o'clock Braddock gave up hope. The white sash he wore made him a conspicuous target and he had been under fire all afternoon. Four horses fell dead under him. With his army demoralized, he sent Washington to advise the various captains to retreat. Washington had hardly left his side before Braddock was hit. A bullet passed through an arm and penetrated the lung. According to one account his soldiers took off his sash and used it as a litter in which to carry him. When they came to the abandoned wagons, they placed him on a two-wheeled tumbrel.

The British were by that time running in wild disorder. The Virginians and the Pennsylvania axmen brought up the rear, retreating from tree to tree and shooting at times. At the river crossing Washington took command of the Virginians and made a stand until the wounded could be got across.

Of Braddock's 1451 men who had crossed that river at noon, 456 were left dead on the field and a dozen were taken prisoner. Of those who escaped 421 were wounded. This left only 562 unhit. Of the 855 led out by Beaujeu, seven French and Canadians and 15 Indians were killed. The number of wounded was about the same.

The fact that Braddock left Dunbar with half the army behind has been criticized by some British strategists, but British and American officers who were present were of the opinion that the slaughter would have been greater had there been more men for the French and Indians to shoot at. Had all of the British officers died at the outset of the Battle, Washington, Stephen, or Waggoner might have won a victory. There was a time, just after Beaujeu's death, when not more than 300 French and Indians were engaged. A well-directed attack, fighting from tree to tree, would have driven the enemy out of the gullies.

While Braddock was at fault in not adapting himself to forest warfare, the enemy also had its weakness. Dumas could not organize a pursuit. As the English were retreating in utter confusion, he could have followed on the flanks, killing them to the last man. The Indians, however, had been promised booty. In order that no one might get more than his share, they gave up pursuit, after Washington organized a defense at the lower crossing of the Monongahela, and set to taking scalps, stripping the dead, and looting the wagons.

And so the disheveled mob that fled from the field, throwing away coats, hats, and guns so they could run faster, escaped. As they ran past the tumbrel in which Braddock was lying, he averted his eyes in shame. But he looked on the Virginians and axmen with approval.

He complimented Washington for organizing the rear guard and directed that he ride after Gage and bring him back. Washington found Gage at the upper crossing, but the officer, who had but 80 men left of the 300 he roused from sleep that morning, declared that if he tried to turn his men back they would refuse to obey. Washington, knowing this to be true, reported back to Braddock.

The general then directed that a camp be put in a defensive position at the upper crossing, where the men would make a stand at least for the night and possibly until Dunbar could come with reinforcements. He directed Washington to ride to Dunbar and direct him to come swiftly. The general could ill spare his only aide, but whom could he trust besides Washington to get through?

Accompanied by Croghan, Washington rode into the failing light. It was the dark of the moon, and the two messengers had only dim starshine sifting through the branches that overhung the 12-foot roadway. All night they rode, blundering amid stumps. At times their horses stepped on soldiers, some wounded and dying, lying in the dirt where they had fallen from exhaustion. Years later Washington wrote: "The shocking scenes which presented themselves are not to be described — the dead — the dying — the groans — the lamentations and cries of the wounded . . . were enough to pierce a heart of adamant. The gloom and horror was not a little increased by impervious darkness occasioned by close shade of the thick woods."

The next day at noon Washington and Croghan came to Dunbar. That officer was frightened half out of his wits. A mounted wagoner had come earlier, declaring he was the sole survivor. Other wagoners arriving later disproved that, but they brought other harrowing details. Washington was able to assure Dunbar that the French had been unable to follow up their victory. He doubted that they would, since they had no wagon train to carry supplies.

Dunbar recovered a little courage and led his men to meet Braddock, while Washington, completely exhausted, rested where he was. Survivors continued straggling in. Burton, Orme, and Morris arrived in litters formed by swinging two poles between two horses and stretching blankets from pole to pole. Braddock rode that way for a time, but the agony became so great that it was necessary to carry him on a litter borne on the shoulders of four men.

When he arrived at Washington's bivouac, it was evident that he was near death. That night he remarked to an officer, "Who would have thought it?" Later he said, "We will know better how to deal with them the next time." He lapsed into unconsciousness and died the fourth night after the battle.

The next morning Washington chose a burial place in the middle of the road at the head of the column. The chaplain was too severely wounded to officiate at the funeral. Dunbar and the lesser British officers did not know how. Washington had buried men both at Jumonville Glen and at Necessity. He drew a prayer book from his baggage and read the Anglican service containing the words: "I am the Resurrection and the Life."

He directed the lowering of the shrouded body into the grave, after which Dunbar took command, directing that every wagon tire, every horse's hoof, every man's foot should march over the grave, pounding down the mound to level it and obliterate it. No epitaph was written. Not even a tree was blazed to mark the place. Otherwise a passing Indian would dig up the grave for its graying scalp and resplendent uniform. Under the ruts of the wagon wheels they left him.

In that forgotten place the general slept until 1824, and only the yowl of the catamount offended his solitude. Then, when workmen were grading for a new road, they excavated human bones. With them they found the metal insignia of a British general and knew they had accidentally dug up Braddock's grave. They reburied the bones nearby and today a monument marks his grave. Thousands of travelers on U. S. Highway 40 pause there, remembering him not for glory he had won at Culloden but for his inglorious defeat at the Battle of the Monongahela. With all of his blunders, he was brave.

Dunbar, before retreating, commanded that all stores be destroyed. This included 150 wagons, many of them valuable. They included wagons that Franklin had obtained from the Pennsylvania farmers, and for whose return he had given his pledge. For a time Franklin was threatened with financial disaster on account of the failure to return the wagons. Eventually Governor Shirley of Massachusetts became commander-in-chief in America and ordered the bill paid.

When Dunbar reached Cumberland, Washington rested a few days and wrote several letters. He assured his mother that he was well and would see her soon. Then like the Mingo chieftain, he attributed his deliverance to a higher power. To Jack he wrote: "By the all-powerful dispensation of Providence I have been protected beyond all human probability or expectation."

The Mingo and Washington were not alone in this thought. The Reverend Samuel Davies, an Episcopal clergyman of Hanover County, Virginia, in a sermon said: "May I point out to the public that heroic youth Colonel Washington, whom I cannot but hope Providence has hitherto preserved in so signal a manner for some important service to his country."*

---

* Quotation from Samuel Davies is from Sparks, *The Writings of Washington.*

XVI. *The Spoils of Victory*

THE depths of depression that prevailed at Fort Cumberland after the harrowing defeat were counterbalanced by the heights of elation at Fort Duquesne. James Smith, the Pennsylvania axman, was a witness to this. The French knew there was no danger of his trying to escape, for to escape meant almost certain capture by the Indians, and capture meant torture.

Smith, therefore, had the freedom of Fort Duquesne, which confined him as effectually as a barbed wire enclosure and mounted guards. From a loft Smith spent the day of July 9 watching and listening for tidings of the battle. In late afternoon the Indians came romping and whooping into the clearing around the fort, and it required no second glance to tell him that the prayer of his heart had received an unfavorable response.

Out of the forest came an Osage warrior flaunting a dripping scalp and wearing a scarlet officer's coat, all gaudy with gilt braid and epaulettes. He was drunk with glory. All their lives the Osages remained proud of having participated in Braddock's defeat, as Lieutenant Zebulon Pike was to learn 51 years later. Pike, on his journey to the Rockies, which was to earn for him an immortal monument, none less than Pike's Peak, stopped on his exploring expedition to visit the Osages. There he was told by Wet Stone, an Osage chief, of his part in the battle.

Also coming from the battlefield was a Maumee warrior carrying an illustrated copy of the "Works of William Shakespeare." Eight years later a Captain Morris of the British army

115

116 THE HORSEMAN OF THE SHENANDOAH

visited a wigwam of the Maumees in what is now northwest Ohio and saw this book in the hands of the same unlettered warrior, who gloated over the illustrations.

Other Indians were carrying scalps, muskets, bayonets, sabers, haversacks, canteens, books, and clothing. They were bloody with the ooze from the scalps. Some wore grenadier caps on their heads. Others wore uniforms or carried boots. Some rode horses. Others, not knowing how to mount the steeds that shied from their naked captors, were leading the beasts.

And now Smith saw twelve British captives, naked and shoeless, their untanned bodies ghastly white against a background of bronzed savages. Their feet were cut and bleeding from having walked for seven miles on thorns and rocks. Like sheep they were driven by the victors past the fort into and across the Allegheny River, which was easily forded because of the drouth.

Just opposite the fort, where Smith had an unimpeded view, the Indians built fires. The Frenchmen watched with indifference as the Indians blackened the faces of the captives, burned them by touching firebrands to their skin, or gashed their muscles, poured powder into the gashes and touched it off. They drove pine needles into their eyeballs and splinters under the fingernails until Smith heard them scream in a most "doleful manner."

"It seemed," reported Smith, "as if Hell had given a holiday and turned loose its inhabitants on the world. As this scene seemed too shocking for me to behold, I retired to my lodgings both sore and sorry."*

---

* Quotations from Smith are from his own narrative published in 1799 and reprinted with notes by William M. Darlington, as *An Account of the Remarkable Occurrences in the Life and Travels of Col. James Smith, During His Captivity with the Indians in the Years 1755–1759*, Cincinnati, Robert Clarke & Co., 1870.

A French officer consoled him by presenting a copy of *Russell's Seven Sermons*. Smith, an adherent to the Stoneite denomination, trying to shut out the horror of the torture fire, read the sermons, which had been taken from a British officer's kit by the Frenchman.

The French had more of an eye for military stores than did the Indians. They wheeled Gage's cannon to Fort Duquesne and brought in wagons loaded with valuable stores, including £25,000 in silver and gold coin. One French soldier came upon Braddock's field cabinet. Unable to read the papers inside, he turned it over to Dumas. That night the French officers gathered in Contrecoeur's headquarters, while an officer with a smattering of English began reading the papers.

He had not read far when he came upon an exact sketch of Fort Duquesne. Accompanying the sketch was a letter to Governor Dinwiddie signed by Stobo.

"What?" exclaimed an officer. "Espionage!"

Contrecoeur ordered Stobo brought before him. This man had violated the freedom that had been accorded him as a hostage. The penalty for such a crime was death. Stobo, however, boasted that he would gladly have died had Braddock taken Fort Duquesne. Contrecoeur proved that the age of chivalry yet lived. He sent both Stobo and Van Braam to Quebec, where they no longer could spy on Duquesne.

There the resourceful Stobo contrived to escape. He was recaptured and confined more closely, but despite French vigilance, he escaped again, boarded a British ship in the St. Lawrence, and presented the British officers with a detailed plan of Quebec and its environs. Van Braam later was allowed to return to England. He never again saw Virginia or Washington.

In Braddock's cabinet Contrecoeur also found complete plans of the English. These Contrecoeur dispatched to Vaudreuil, who directed a force to meet Shirley. This compelled the

Area of the war in the North

Massachusetts governor to dig in at the site of the present Oswego, where he built Fort Ontario at the southeast corner of Lake Ontario and 150 miles short of Fort Niagara. Shirley left a garrison of 500 men at Fort Ontario and returned to Boston for the winter, intending to continue the advance on Niagara in the spring.

Vaudreuil ordered Baron Dieskau to meet Johnson. The two armies fought at the end of Lake George, where St. Pierre, an officer under Dieskau, who had been host to Washington at Le Boeuf, was killed. Dieskau was wounded and taken prisoner. Johnson, too, was wounded and his army stalemated. The British ministry, pleased that Johnson did no worse, had the king knight him. Henceforth he was Sir William Johnson and his Mohawk wife became Lady Johnson.

As for the prisoner, James Smith, the French eventually surrendered him to a tribe of Canadian Indians. He lived with them so long that, after he escaped and returned to Pennsylvania in 1760, his gait and gesture were so like an Indian's that his own parents did not recognize him. He inquired for his sweetheart to learn she had been married to another only a few days before his return. Commented Smith: "It is impossible now for me to describe the emotion of (correct) foul I felt."

Going back to the evening of the battle on the Monongahela Field, we could have seen the French and Indians burying their dead. They carried Perade and Beaujeu to Fort Duquesne and buried them in the yard of the Chapel of the Assumption of the Blessed Virgin at the Beautiful River. In the burial records Beaujeu is referred to as commander of Fort Duquesne. In fact, Contrecoeur had asked to be relieved of command and Beaujeu had been sent to replace him, with instructions that Contrecoeur, who was ill, should remain as commander at the fort and Beaujeu, the field commander until after the battle.

Over the field commander's grave they erected a wooden cross, but a few years later people came to whom a wooden cross was so much kindling and the cross disappeared. Today nothing marks the resting place of the man who planned the victory on the Monongahela.

On the Monongahela battlefield no prayers were whispered to ease the passage of the dead English into another world. But after the victors had taken the plunder from the field, the shadowy gray wolves skulked to the sides of the scalped and naked soldiers and howled a requiem.

Through the summer wild beasts and carrion birds worried the bones, but they left the body of Ensign James Halkett where he fell across the body of his father. With the coming of autumn compassionate nature gently spread a soft coverlet of fragrant leaves — yellow, bronze, brown, gold, and red — over the whitening skeletons.

XVII. *They Harry the Frontier*

SHORTLY after the Battle of the Monongahela Contrecoeur turned the command of Fort Duquesne over to Dumas. The new captain sent small parties of Indians, usually with a French officer, to harry the frontier. Braddock's Road made it easy for them to go all the way to Fort Cumberland, where they sometimes shot at the English there.

The battle regenerated the Delawares. No longer did they admit they were women. They harangued each other over their wrongs. They told how they had been defrauded out of Pennsylvania and cried for revenge. Captain Jacobs now spurned pacifism and neutrality and took the French side. Having been born in eastern Pennsylvania, he knew the country as did hundreds of others. They knew every secret path, every hiding place, every hollow tree, and every natural grotto.

They went as far east as the Walking Treaty country, hiding in the thickets and listening to what the English said. They killed families when they felt like it, and supplied themselves with powder and new firearms by capturing them from the English.

The governor begged the British officers for aid, but Dunbar was in no mood to aid anybody. Washington, still convalescing at Fort Cumberland, found that Dunbar was about to abandon that fort. Since Washington was an aide to Braddock and Braddock was dead, he no longer had any place in the army. He therefore wrote as a civilian to Governor Dinwiddie, telling what Dunbar intended.

The governor wrote to Dunbar, urging that he attack the

French at Fort Duquesne. He still had 2000 men, but he had burned his stores and wagons. For answer Dunbar retreated to Philadelphia, leaving the sick and wounded at Cumberland to contrive their own defense. As soon as he could arrange passage he put the Atlantic Ocean between himself and the terrors of the Ohio.

Washington returned to Mount Vernon to help Jack manage the farm. He had plenty of time to reflect that he had done better than any of the British officers. He and other American colonial soldiers learned that they were just as brave, just as hardy, and at least the equal in generalship of any British officer they had seen.

Scarouady, the Mingo chief, who had succeeded to the position of Half King, also weighed the British and found them wanting. He addressed the governor and the Pennsylvania council, urging them to do their own fighting. Scarouady had remained loyal to the British despite Braddock. He had fought at the Battle of the Monongahela and knew from firsthand that the British, while brave, did not know how to fight in the woods. "Let us go ourselves," he implored, "we that came out of the ground."

All fall the raiding continued. The Indians burned so many cabins that their smoke was continually in the air. The Wyandottes, whose tribe had been decimated by the Iroquois a century before, began rebuilding their numbers by stealing children in Virginia and Pennsylvania. They killed the adults and children who cowered from them, but boys and girls with spirit they carried away. When the war ended, some of these children were recovered but enough were retained to change the complexion of the Wyandotte tribe. The Wyandottes of Kansas and Oklahoma today have distinctive Caucasian features. Many have blue or gray eyes, although they proudly claim to be Indians.

So destructive were the Indian raids that in the fall, Dumas bragged to Vaudreuil: "The enemy has lost more since the battle than on the day of the defeat of Braddock."*

Deserted by Dunbar, the Burgesses met to vote money for defense. Speaker Robinson and other Burgesses wanted Washington to be commander. Dinwiddie, remembering that Washington had resigned the year before, foresaw more quarrels as Washington insisted that he would not take orders from king's officers of lower rank. The governor thought it would be better to appoint Innes, who had a king's commission as well as a North Carolina commission. Friends of Washington urged him to come to Williamsburg to volunteer his services. But he held aloof. To his half brother, Austin, who was a Burgess, he wrote: "I was employed to go on a journey in the winter, when, I believe, few or none would have undertaken it — and what did I get by it? My expenses borne! I then was appointed, with trifling pay, to conduct a handful of men to the Ohio. What did I get by that? Why, after putting myself to a considerable expense, in equipping and providing necessaries for the campaign, I went out, was soundly beaten, and lost them all! — came in, and had my commission taken from me, or, in other words, had my command reduced."

He clarified his position further by writing his mother: "If the command is pressed upon me, by the general voice of the country, and offered upon such terms as cannot be objected against, it would reflect dishonor on me to refuse it."

In the end, after the Burgesses voted to raise 1000 men in addition to the 200 that remained in the service, Dinwiddie bowed to popular will and named Washington commander-in-chief of all forces raised or to be raised in Virginia. He

* Translations from Dumas and other French officers in this and later chapters are from Francis Parkman, *Montcalm and Wolfe* (Boston: Little Brown & Co., 1884).

agreed that Washington could name his own subordinate officers, except such captains and lieutenants as Dinwiddie already had commissioned. Washington's title should be colonel.

Washington accepted. He promoted Adam Stephen to second in command with the rank of lieutenant colonel. He named Andrew Lewis major; Captain George Mercer aide; and Captain Robert Stewart, who with another officer had carried Braddock from the field on his sash, secretary.

Washington liked to be honored, but he was embarrassed when news came from England of the adulation he and his Virginians received there. A London newspaper declared that the Virginians held the Monongahela battlefield for three hours after the British had fled and credited Washington with their leadership. Copies of the British papers came to America and the story was reprinted in Philadelphia. Washington knew that the Virginians had acted bravely, but he blushed at the exaggeration.

He had little time for blushing. He established headquarters at Winchester in the same building he had used as his office when he was a boy surveyor for Lord Fairfax. The surrounding area, which had been a wilderness with a few clearings when he first came there, was now a settled community with a stretch of farms for miles about. Settlements extended southwest for fifty miles into Augusta County and westward beyond the south fork of the Potomac.

Hundreds of families, to avoid rents and taxes, had crossed the Alleghenies to settle in secluded mountain coves on Tygart's Fork and the Great Kanawha. Such pioneers were as sitting quail to the Indians, who could approach under the forest covert, kill a farmer in his corn patch, tomahawk his wife, and carry off his children if they were pleasing.

The settlers were too far apart to support each other and too far removed to be protected by troops. The survivors of the raids picked up their belongings and fled to Winchester, spreading tales of death and creating a panic. Washington informed Dinwiddie: "I have invited the poor distressed people, who were driven from their habitations, to lodge their families in some place of security, and join our parties in scouring the woods. I believe some will cheerfully assist."

A few assisted, but most men knew that if they joined the army, their families would be left destitute. The enemy, emboldened, invaded the Shenandoah Valley. Soon families were in flight out of the valley itself, congesting roads that crossed the Blue Ridge to the older portions of Virginia.

"Captain Waggoner informs me," so Washington reported to the governor, "that it was with difficulty he passed the Ridge, for crowds of people, were flying as if every moment was death."

As the corn ripened in October, Washington tried to persuade farmers with wagons to harvest it under guards of soldiers, but few farmers responded. The corn remained where it was. Hogs, abandoned when the settlers fled, broke down some of the stalks for feed. All fall and the following spring the standing corn and the surviving pigs afforded a ready-filled pantry for the enemy.

Washington directed the building of stockade forts, garrisoning each with a few men and depending on added help from settlers who would take refuge there. Altogether Washington was short of men. Recruiting was slow. Even after a man volunteered, he might desert.

Parties sent out to find the elusive enemy were mostly ineffectual. One party did bring back a French officer's scalp, which Washington sent to Dinwiddie. Usually the Indians from Fort Duquesne struck and ran to their covert. To chase them was like "sending a cow to catch a rabbit."

Winter and snow brought respite. In bad weather the Indians kept to their wigwams, recounting their exploits and teaching captive white children how to become savages.

Winter also brought opportunity to settle an annoying condition. Washington stationed Colonel Stephen at Fort Cumberland, where at first he was the sole commandant. In mid-autumn Governor Sharpe of Maryland sent Captain John Dagworthy with 30 men to Cumberland. Now Cumberland is on the Maryland side of the Potomac, although it was stocked with provisions from Virginia.

Dagworthy held a king's commission dated 1746. It had lapsed, and his present commission was signed by Governor Sharpe, but Dagworthy had presented the king's commission to Braddock and Braddock had placed Dagworthy over all colonial officers and even over British captains with later commissions.

Dagworthy claimed to outrank Stephen and even forbade him to draw rations from the Virginia stores without a requisition on the Maryland captain. He also forbade the Virginians to turn out the guard to salute Washington when he came to inspect the Virginia troops. Sharpe backed up Dagworthy in his pretensions. Dinwiddie sided with Washington and Stephen. He appealed to Governor Shirley, who since the death of Braddock, was the ranking general in America.

Shirley wrote to Sharpe, advising him that since Dagworthy's king's commission had expired, he was but a colonial officer with no rank over Washington or Stephen. Shirley, however, sent no copy of the letter to Dinwiddie. Sharpe notified Dagworthy, but since the Virginians knew nothing of the letter, Dagworthy continued to claim authority.

With winter coming on, Washington appealed to Dinwiddie for permission to call on Shirley in Boston. This meant a winter ride, but winter had no terrors for the man who had ridden to Le Boeuf. He traveled in style, taking with him

Captain Mercer and Captain Stewart and two Negro slaves dressed in livery. Of course nobody made a finer figure on a horse than Washington. Everywhere he attracted attention as he rode into Philadelphia, New York, Boston, and other cities with his retinue. A forecast of what he might expect was sent to Washington by Gist some months earlier. While on a military mission to Philadelphia, Gist wrote to Washington: "Your name is more talked of than of any other person in the army."

Washington visited the governor at Philadelphia and also at New York. In New York he called on Beverly Robinson, brother of the Speaker of the Virginia House. Robinson was a New York businessman, married to Susannah Philipse, an heiress. At Robinson's house George met Susannah's unmarried sister Mary, whom Washington escorted to a musical program and a show in Exposition Hall. She owned 51,000 acres of land, but Washington was not interested in becoming her suitor.

New York and Philadelphia were cities of more than 3000 houses, the greatest cities the Virginians had seen. In Boston, also a greater city than any in Virginia, the governor treated Washington with great courtesy. He inquired about the death of his son who had been secretary to Braddock, and Washington was able to report that the young man had displayed great courage under fire and had died bravely.

When Washington presented the reason for his visit, Shirley expressed astonishment that Sharpe had not curbed the impudent captain. He was so angered, in fact, that he took nearly a week to cool off as he pondered a suitable reply. Meanwhile, the colonel and his captains were entertained by Boston's best society. Washington also sat for a portrait by John Singleton Copley, age 19, who had not yet risen to fame. To be suitably dressed for Boston, he spent 12 pounds, 10 shillings for a "Hatt"; 95 pounds, 7 shillings, and 3 pence for a "Taylor";

94 pounds, 17 shillings, and 1 pence for silver lace; and 1 pound, 18 shillings, and 1 pence for gloves. This was paid in Massachusetts paper currency, valued at about one-ninth that of Virginia currency, which was backed with tobacco.

Fitted in a red coat with red buttons, a ruffled silver lace shirt with white stock, he made a dashing appearance. His companions also were suitably garbed. When they rode through the streets attended by two black men in livery, Bostonians craned their necks.

At length Shirley handed Washington a letter with instruction to deliver it in person to Governor Sharpe. He had a copy made for Washington to deliver to Dinwiddie. It read: "Captain Dagworthy . . . can only take the rank of a provincial Captain and is of course under the command of all field officers, and, in case it should happen that Colonel Washington and Captain Dagworthy should join at Fort Cumberland, it is my order that Colonel Washington shall take command."

He sent a second letter to Governor Sharpe, telling him to instruct Dagworthy either to quit making trouble or be withdrawn from Fort Cumberland. Washington lost no time in hurrying back to Virginia by the way of Baltimore, where he delivered the letters to Sharpe. He arrived in Williamsburg March 30 after an absence of two months.

He had scarcely arrived when news came of more Indian raids in the Shenandoah. He was in for another season of disheartening guerrilla war, but he no longer had to contend with the arrogance of Dagworthy.

XVIII. *While Generals Blunder*

THE gratitude glowing in Washington's heart toward his commander-in-chief for putting Dagworthy in his place was soon dimmed a bit. Shirley's diagram for war against France in 1756 omitted all reference to Fort Duquesne. In a letter to Dinwiddie, Washington urged an attack on Fort Duquesne first. He commented: "I have always thought it the best and only method to put a stop to the incursions of the enemy, as they would then be obliged to stay at home to defend their own possessions."

Dinwiddie, Sharpe, and Hamilton urged Shirley to reconsider, but the general believed that by taking Fort Niagara, he would pinch off water communication between Montreal and interior America. Then the French no longer could send gifts from Canada to the Ohio Indians. Stop the gifts, and the loyalty of the Indians for France would wither. He overlooked the growing interest of the Indians in war. They were finding it exhilarating and profitable and were engaging in it with zest for its own sake.

Shirley pushed forward his design to take Niagara with vigor. He established headquarters at Albany and began mobilizing New England and New York troops there before the spring sap was rising in the trees. From Albany to Fort Ontario he had to travel a wilderness waterway up the Mohawk to a portage and down the Oswego River to its mouth where Fort Ontario stood on the site of the present city of Oswego. The distance was 200 miles in a bee line, but much farther by the winding river channels.

In charge of transporting troops and supplies he commissioned one of the unsung heroes of the time, Captain John Bradstreet, a native of Nova Scotia, who had fought in King George's War and had been a prisoner for a time. He was a supreme master at building the flat-bottom bateaux, needed on the rivers he would traverse, and held the unbounded confidence of his bateauxmen.

It was necessary for reinforcements to go to Fort Ontario with speed, for the garrison was in a desperate plight. Had Vaudreuil known its condition, he could have captured it with a small force. After Shirley left the 500 men at Fort Ontario the fall before, some of them, feeling secure in their double-logged buildings, sent for their families, and about 200 women and children joined them.

The men began building ships of green lumber in a cove on the lake, for Shirley intended to move the 150 miles from Fort Ontario to Fort Niagara across Lake Ontario, thereby avoiding an ambuscade in the forest. The men were directed by master ship's carpenters, and they proceeded with their construction program until after winter locked the rivers and lakes with deep ice, and cutting winds screeched over Lake Ontario to drift snow about the fort.

The snow buried rabbits and other game in their burrows and warrens, cutting off the supply of ready food for the timber wolves, which grew gaunt and added their laments to the roar of the wind. Then sickness came. Nursing mothers were the first to succumb. Lacking antiscorbutic vitamins, they had to draw the elements from their own bodies to feed their babies. Their gums grew sore. Their faces became haggard. Their teeth fell out. It was scurvy. The babies and men also fell victims. Then came dysentery. At times there were as few as sixteen men fit to walk the sentry beats. "Men were so weak the sentries often fell down at their posts," wrote an officer. The children who survived whimpered constantly; even after they had eaten and were filled they were still hungry for the food lacked vitamins.

Never did men await spring with greater longing. It came on the wings of northering waterfowl. By that time one half of the garrison was lying in graves chopped into the frozen earth by men almost too weak to raise a pick. Green leaf buds and nettles cooked for greens stopped the scurvy, but dysentery still prevailed.

When the rivers were open Bradstreet and his bateauxmen came to Fort Ontario with 1600 men and ample supplies. With 400 bateauxmen Bradstreet started to return to Albany, taking out the women and children and the hopelessly ill.

From concealment Villiers, the victor at Fort Necessity, watched their departure. With Canadians and Indians at his heels he trailed the flotilla up the Oswego River until they came to a shallows where it was necessary to lighten the bateaux and carry them. It was just the spot for Villiers, who spread his men through the woods and attacked from both sides at once.

This time he was not dealing with men in water-filled trenches as at Necessity. Neither was he opposing men led by a Braddock. At the very first warwhoop Bradstreet set an example by taking to the cover of a tree, ordering his men to do likewise. Fighting from tree to tree, the bateauxmen sent Villiers reeling back to Canada. Returning to Albany the victorious Bradstreet was filling his bateaux with supplies for a second voyage. Shirley had a second army ready to embark.

Not only that, he had Indians. Early in the spring Sir William Johnson assembled the Iroquois headmen in his home at Fort Johnson on the Mohawk and persuaded them to join in Shirley's campaign against Fort Niagara. As Shirley's army would move on Lake Ontario by ship and bateaux, the Indians would move alongside, following the tangled forest trails on the south side of the lake. Bradstreet's victory swung the Indians to the English side.

Then Johnson presented a new idea. Why should redmen fight redmen? Why not make an alliance with the Delawares and Shawnees? The Iroquois agreed and met the Indians from the Ohio in June on Lake Onondaga. There the Iroquois, acting on the advice of Johnson, greeted the Delawares and Shawnees as equals and brothers. Johnson went through the ceremony of stripping off a dress from a Delaware, thereby showing that the English and Iroquois agreed that the Delawares no longer were women but men, fit to fight alongside the Iroquois. By diplomacy Johnson had won an army of Indians. It looked as though Shirley's campaign was certain of success.

But Shirley, instead of issuing from Albany, found himself stymied by events across the sea. In May, 1756, King George's government, after having fought France for two years, decided to declare a state of war. This was the fourth conflict between France and England in 60 years. In England it is known as the Seven Years' War. In American history books it is the French and Indian War.

The king was a German by birth and spoke German better than English. He had a sentimental regard for his native Hanover far outweighing his interest in his overseas domains. And Hanover was in danger. George, therefore, led his ministers into an alliance with Frederick the Great of Prussia to defend Hanover.

Frederick was a glutton for trouble. He had alienated Maria Theresa, empress of Austria. Then he insulted his natural ally, Elizabeth, empress of Russia. Not content with quarreling with two women rulers, he sneered at Madame Pompadour, who had no office at all but was mistress of King Louis XV, autocrat of France, and through Louis made war on Frederick. Sweden and Saxony joined the three women to destroy Frederick. England cast its lot with the Prussian king and for seven years sent armies to die in Germany.

Few British troops could be spared for America but the king's war minister sent as commander-in-chief 52-year-old John Campbell, Earl of Loudon, who also succeeded Albemarle as governor of Virginia. Like Albemarle he left the governing to Dinwiddie, the lieutenant governor. Second in command under Loudon was Major General James Abercromby, who proceeded to Albany and ordered Shirley to go to New York and confer with Loudon. Shirley told Abercromby and later Loudon that he had an army ready to go to Fort Ontario and it was needed there, but the two British generals let Shirley find out that they were running the show. Shirley retired to Boston to exercise his duties as governor. He soon was removed from that post and ordered back to England where he was investigated for treason. He was cleared, partly because he had lost his eldest son in the Braddock campaign and another had died of disease at Fort Ontario. To the English courts a man who had given two sons to his country could hardly rate as a traitor.

The Delawares and Shawnees waited for a time, but as Bradstreet and the army lingered at Albany, Ohio Indians grew tired of the delay and returned to their raids on Pennsylvania. Loudon, after conferring with the governors of Pennsylvania, Maryland, Virginia, and North Carolina, turned down their requests for a march on Duquesne. He arrived in Albany late in July, where he had 10,000 men assembled under Abercromby to march against Fort Ticonderoga. He decided to throw all of his force in that direction, except a detachment under Bradstreet, which departed for Fort Ontario on August 12, not to take Niagara, but to hold Ontario until the following year.

The French, too, had a new general. After the capture of Dieskau the year before, Vaudreuil had been in command of France in America. But early in the spring the French ministry named Louis Joseph, Marquis de Montcalm, as commander-in-chief. The new French leader arrived in May, bringing more regular soldiers. He now had 3000 disciplined French regulars and 16,000 Canadian militia. The militia served without pay, marched without tents, trusting to hastily built half-faced huts of bark for shelter from storm. They were poorly disciplined, but well schooled to love France, revere their king, and worship God. They could subsist, when necessary, by hunting and fishing alone. Montcalm also had Indians who fought when they felt like it and sometimes carried information to the enemy. The Indians were a novelty to Montcalm. To his mother he wrote: "The men always carry to war, along with their tomahawk and gun, a mirror to daub their faces with various colors, and arrange feathers on their heads and rings in their ears and noses."

A French officer, writing of the Indians, said: "It is incredible the quantity of scalps they bring us. In Virginia they have committed unheard of cruelties, carried off families, burned a great many houses, and killed an infinity of people. These miserable English are in the extremity of distress, and repent too late the unjust war they began against us. It is a pleasure to make war in Canada."

Montcalm was at Fort Ticonderoga, called Carillon by the French, when he saw how slowly the English were moving. Leaving 3000 men to defend Ticonderoga, he directed the rest to follow him in canoes. Down Lake Champlain and down the Richelieu River they boomed, taking shifts at the paddles

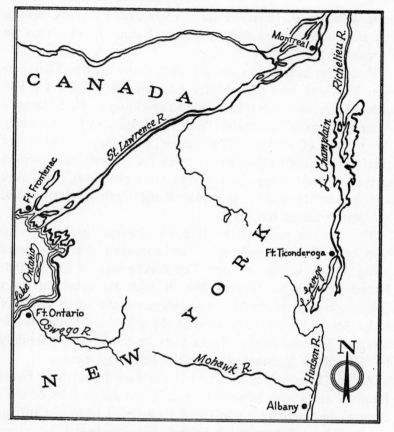

Water courses followed by Montcalm

so that they might sleep in turns and voyage day and night.

At the mouth of the Richelieu they entered the St. Lawrence and headed up stream, bucking the tide until on August 4 they were in the woods surrounding Fort Ontario. The French mounted cannon and captured the three log buildings of the fort one at a time. Montcalm received the surrender of 1600 men. Despite his efforts to protect his prisoners, the Indians massacred a part of the force. Montcalm's men leveled the forts with fire. A priest erected a cross over the ruins. With a hot iron he engraved these words in Latin, "By this sign we conquered."

Four days later Montcalm was on his way back to Ticonderoga. This was four days before Loudon, on August 12, had ordered Bradstreet to take a relief expedition to Fort Ontario. After the victory Montcalm's Indians abandoned him to dance the tidings of victory. The farther west they voyaged the greater grew their tales. By the time the Menominee warriors arrived at their village in the Wisconsin pinelands, they were saying that Montcalm, "trampler of the English," was so tall his head bumped the sky.

The disaster stunned the Iroquois. Invited by Johnson to help take Fort Ticonderoga, they answered that they were going to watch this one out. The disaffection of the Indians forced Loudon to content himself with strengthening Fort William Henry, begun the year before on the south shore of Lake George, and Fort Edward on the Hudson, 14 miles to the south of William Henry. These forts he garrisoned, intending to make them his starting place the following spring.

Among Loudon's provincial officers were John Stark, Israel Putnam, and Philip Schuyler who saw the deficiencies of their commanders and were convinced they could whip the British in war. These three men all became generals in the American Revolution and had a chance to test out their belief.

As for the private soldiers, they referred to Abercromby as Nabby Cromby. Nabby was New Englandese for Abby or Abigail, a nice name for a girl.

Encouraged by the blundering of the British generals, the Indians, accompanied by French officers, moved in small parties to raid the English settlements as they had the year before. Scalping parties came within a dozen miles of Winchester. "The inhabitants," reported Washington, "are so apprehensive that I believe, unless we stop the depradations of the Indians, the Blue Ridge will soon become our frontier."

The Burgesses voted money to build forts and authorized 2000 men, but the most Washington ever had at one time that summer was 925 scouts, rangers, and soldiers. He scattered the soldiers among 27 forts that were built that year and the next. Rangers tried to intercept French and Indian raiding parties in the forest and occasionally did so.

The Indians attacked one of the forts and were beaten off with such loss that they left the other forts alone. The forts were designed as rallying points to which farmers might fly for refuge in time of attack. Washington sent Major Lewis to raid an Indian village on the Ohio, but when the major neared the place, his scouts brought reports of such enemy strength that he retired without offering battle.

All that year and the next Washington rode the trails from one fort to another. Murder lurked in the shadows. Once he rode into an ambush, but rode out again unhit. Thus again the legend grew that Providence was sparing him for a greater mission.

XIX. *Pennsylvania Sheds Pacifism*

THE plight of Virginia was bad, but Washington's frontier regiment at least confined Indian irruptions to the counties west of the Blue Ridge. Pennsylvania, on the other hand, lay defenseless before the scalping knife. Occasional predators even penetrated as far as the Delaware River east of Bethlehem, a region from which the Delaware Indians had been ejected by Thomas Penn's agents 14 years before.

Of course it was the frontier west of the Susquehanna that suffered most. This territory was settled to a large extent by Scotch-Irish Presbyterians from Ulster, who had been placed there as a buffer to protect the Friends settlements of southeast Pennsylvania. Some writers, either through ignorance or disrespect for the truth, have asserted that the Friends enjoyed immunity from war because the Indians revered their pacifism.

James Logan, a prominent Friend, who served as confidential secretary and manager for William Penn and later in the same capacity for William's son, Thomas, had no such illusions. He told in a letter written in 1729 why he built a rampart of Scotch-Irish to the west of the Friends settlements. His explanation reads: "About this time considerable numbers of good sober people came in from Ireld who wanted to be settled, at ye same time also it happened that we were under some apprehension from ye northern Indians. . . . I therefore thought it might be prudent to plant a settlement of such men as those who had so bravely defended Derry and Innskillen, as a frontier in case of Disturbance. Accordingly ye township of Donegal was settled."* By 1729 Logan had 6000 Scotch-Irish in the western settlements. By 1736 he had 17,000.

When the Indian wars broke, the suffering Westerners demanded of the Pennsylvania Assembly a military law requiring all of the colony to participate in defense. Unfortunately the Assembly was quarreling with Robert H. Morris, who had replaced Hamilton as governor, over the right to tax the lands owned by Thomas Penn.

Penn was the chief proprietor of the colony. He leased land at very small rent to the farmers and contended that the king's grant to his father permitted no taxation. The governor was appointed on recommendation of the proprietor and, therefore, sided with him. He stood ready to veto any bill that levied a tax on his master.

A greater difficulty was the attitude of the Friends, who had a majority in the Assembly. Answering a demand that they vote for a military law to repel the Indians, they replied: "If they [the Indians] have suffered wrongs, we are resolved to do all in our power to redress them rather than entail upon ourselves and our posterity the calamities of a cruel Indian war."

Later a committee of Friends explained their position in this memorial: "The raising of Money . . . to Purposes in contrast with the Peacable Testimony we profess and have born to the World appears to Us in its Consequences to be Destructive of our Religious Liberties."**

Some of the Delaware warriors from the Ohio, rather than face the tough Scotch-Irish, turned upon the Moravian settlements centering around Bethlehem. These Moravians had origi-

---

* Quotation from Logan's letter is from Charles P. Keith, *Chronicles of Pennsylvania, 1688–1748*, Philadelphia, 1917.
** Quotations from unnamed Friends leader are from Parkman, *Montcalm and Wolfe*.

nally migrated from Moravia into Germany and later to Pennsylvania, because of freedom from military service. Since they were pledged to nonresistance, it was as easy to kill them as to shoot a dove. Ohio Delawares entered one house near Bethlehem and killed several children and the mother before the eyes of the man of the house who did nothing but pray. Then they killed him. One boy, who showed fight, they carried into captivity and brought up as a Delaware.

Next the Ohio Delawares entered the village of Gnaden-Hutten, which can be translated into "gracious homes." In that village lived about 100 Delawares, converts to the Moravian faith, and a few families of white Moravians, who were at the same time farmers and missionaries to their red neighbors. They taught industry as well as peace and love of God to the Indians. It was dusk of late November when the invaders arrived sniffing the fragrance of hams, bacon, and beef curing in the smokehouses. They stole to the house of Joseph Sturges, where 14 people, including Mr. and Mrs. George Partch, newly married, were living with the warmhearted Sturges family until they could build homes of their own.

The household had just listened as Sturges asked the blessing and began to eat supper when the angry snarling of the family dog indicated that strangers were approaching. Sturges threw open the door to welcome visitors, and there he stood, framed in the light cast by the glowing fireplace.

The marauders opened fire, killing three. One bullet hit Sturges in the head but failed to break his skull. Sturges retreated to the loft with part of his household, including Mrs. Partch. Her husband jumped out of a window and escaped to the surrounding timber. Upstairs Sturges slammed a trap door in the faces of the Indians who tried to follow him and put a weight upon it. Thereupon the Indians built a fire in the stairway.

Those in the loft were forced by the smoke to leap through the loft window to the ground and make for the timber where Partch was hiding. Mrs. Partch, afraid of the woods, hid behind a stump where she remained through the night watching the horrid scene by the light of houses fired one after another. Most of the inhabitants, startled by the barking of dogs and gunshots, abandoned their homes to hide in the woods.

Mrs. Partch saw the Indians deliberately moving from house to house, killing any persons that had failed to run.

They took their time, for there was no danger of the Moravians fighting back. Altogether they killed and scalped eleven white persons and about the same number of Moravian Indians. Toward midnight they gathered in the communal springhouse and feasted on meat from the smokehouses. Then Mrs. Partch saw them lead off or kill the horses and cattle as they left Gnaden-Hutten a smoldering ruin.

The next morning Sturges and Partch enlisted the aid of men with muskets and returned to the desolate village where they found Mrs. Partch shivering from cold but otherwise unharmed.

The small loss of life, as compared with that of the frontier settlements, was of no particular consequence, but Gnaden-Hutten was only 50 miles from Philadelphia. Further, the Moravians were pacifists. This showed that part of the Ohio Indians, if not all, had lost respect for men of peace. The Germans south of Philadelphia, who had come to Pennsylvania from their homeland to escape military service, now joined the Scotch-Irish in demanding a militia law. They announced their willingness to raise companies of volunteers.

In December, 1755, a heavy snow covered the colony's dirt roads, making it possible for the Scotch-Irish to drive in sleds to Philadelphia, carrying as their cargo the mutilated and frozen corpses of their neighbors. They stood in front of the

Assembly hall, demanding a military law and cursing the Friends.

Governor Morris resigned in disgust and was succeeded by a former soldier, William Denny. The new governor obtained from Penn a grant of money for defense, given on the condition that he be exempt from taxation. The Assembly postponed a showdown on the question of taxes, while Benjamin Franklin, a 49-year-old Assemblyman, who had a high regard for the Friends and they for him, quoted the ancient adage: "Make yourself a sheep, and the wolves will eat you."

He wrote a militia bill, exempting the Friends and other conscientious objectors from service. He went further and provided that only volunteers need serve. The volunteers should elect their officers and the Assembly should provide pay and arms.

Six of the Friends leaders resigned from the Assembly, thereby giving a majority to the militia party. This permitted the passage of a militia bill, carrying with it an appropriation of £60,000. Franklin, without an election and wholly by common consent, began building forts on the western frontier in 1756. Some were small blockhouses. A few were quite substantial, with sleeping quarters and granaries.

In August, 1756, a band of Delawares attacked one of the smaller forts, took it, and killed the garrison. It was believed that the leader was Captain Jacobs. Having lived part of his life in the Susquehanna Valley, Jacobs had a map of Pennsylvania etched on his brain. He knew the hideouts, knew the frontier settlements, knew the habits of farmers, and knew just where to strike.

He made his headquarters at Kittanning, about halfway between Venango and Fort Duquesne on the Allegheny River. It was a Delaware village of 30 Swedish-style log houses. Jacobs made it the center for forays on the Pennsylvania settlements.

He now resolved to attack Fort Shirley, one of the larger frontier forts a few miles south of the Juniata River. The site is now marked by the city of Shirleysburg. As a convenient calendar he set the time to leave Kittanning as September 9, the date of the full moon, which all the Indians could read.

The Pennsylvanians knew nothing of the plan against Fort Shirley, but it came to the mind of 39-year-old John Armstrong, pioneer farmer and surveyor of Carlisle, that the Ohio Delawares would be more likely to stay at home to defend themselves if an army attacked Kittanning. He won the approval of Governor Denny, who called for volunteers to rendezvous at Fort Shirley. Armstrong raised a company of 100 volunteers at Carlisle and was elected captain. He marched to Fort Shirley where 200 more men were gathered. They elected him commander-in-chief with the rank of lieutenant colonel.

Armstrong laid his plans to strike Kittanning the morning of September 8, or just one day before the full moon. He doubtless selected this time because the full moon in September, which is the harvest moon, rises shortly after sunset for several successive evenings after the moon is full. This would provide light all night for several nights to illuminate their retreat. Further they would have a waxing moon to light them as they neared the village.

The army marched the morning of August 30 with their lieutenant colonel at their head. He knew nothing about the intricate evolutions on a regimental front. He did know that when you see an enemy, you must shoot him and shoot first.

The men had only a smattering of drill, but they were used to shooting squirrels, coons, catamounts, and bears and had confidence in their own marksmanship. They knew there was a risk in marching into the dark woods where Braddock's men had been slaughtered, but they believed there was less risk than in waiting to be killed at home.

The distance from modern Shirleysburg to present-day Kittanning by way of U. S. Highways 22 and 422 is 126 miles. It was farther in 1756 as the men wound over mountain passes, threaded ravines, shouldered through tangled brushland, or strolled across glades. A packtrain carried supplies. If the attack was to succeed, it was necessary to advance without discovery by the Indians. Armstrong, therefore, kept a screen of scouts ahead of his army. At times he paused so that the scouts could reconnoiter and return.

Thirty miles from Kittanning the regiment stopped, built a scaffold, placed food and other supplies upon it out of the reach of bears and wildcats. On the night of September 7, Armstrong left a lieutenant with a small detachment to watch the pack horses. The men who were to accompany Armstrong divested themselves of haversacks and blankets, leaving them to the care of the horse detail.

They were only six miles from Kittanning, and they were going to attack the following daybreak. At 10 o'clock at night they moved by moonlight. The scouts discovered ahead a band of 24 sleeping warriors. Armstrong was tempted to attack and destroy them, but that was risky, for if only one escaped, he would carry a warning to Kittanning. Armstrong, therefore, led his men around the sleeping Delaware camp. He did not know it, but it was an advance party on its way to reconnoiter Fort Shirley.

Before the moon set the Pennsylvanians came to the Allegheny River about 100 yards south of Kittanning. Here most of the men flopped to the ground and fell asleep, but not the scouts. Armstrong sent them to explore the cornfield between the Pennsylvanians and the town. The scouts returned with the alarming information that the field was full of sleeping warriors. This was surprising and disappointing. It meant not only that they could not reach the houses of the village undetected, but they would have to fight a larger force than they expected.

As day began to break, Armstrong quietly roused the men. He divided his command into two parties. He sent a captain with one party around the cornfield to attack directly from the east, while Armstrong would march up from the south. He allowed 20 minutes for the other party to reach its post and begin its march. Then both would advance at the same time.

The encircling party had completed its maneuver and had just commenced its advance when it scared up a sleeping warrior. He raced toward the log houses, shouting lustily. The Pennsylvanians fired on him. Instantly the village was awake as were the bands of Indians in the cornfield and additional bands across the river. The field was all arustle from warriors stirring the corn blades as they ran and with the Pennsylvanians almost on their heels. Muskets barked on both sides. Bullets screamed. A sergeant, terrified, turned and ran, followed by fifteen men. The rest, however, remained steadfast.

A man beside Armstrong was hit and sprawled to the ground dead. Burning lead struck Armstrong in a shoulder. The colonel hesitated long enough for a private soldier to bind the wound with a ribbon taken from his queue. Then Armstrong ran ahead, calling encouragement. The warriors from the cornfield now took refuge in the log houses, which were loopholed for muskets. Since Kittanning had been made the point of Delaware rendezvous, every house was an arsenal with supplies of powder and lead. Jacobs cried out: "The white men have at last come, and we'll have plenty of scalps."

He ordered the women and children to hide in the woods to make room inside the cabins for the warriors, as he knew full well that the white men would not shoot the women and children. Armstrong now called out in English for the Indians to surrender, and such of the Pennsylvanians as could speak Delaware repeated the surrender summons in that tongue. For answer Jacobs yelled back:

"I'm a man and will not be a prisoner."

"You'll be burnt then," threatened the Pennsylvanians.

"Then I'll kill three or four before I die," boasted Jacobs.

Failure to reach the houses undetected put the Pennsylvanians at a disadvantage, for it gave time for the Delawares to get inside where they had the protection of logs. Armstrong, consequently, called for volunteers to fling firebrands on the nearest houses. It was possible to draw near to only a few of the structures, but the fires started there gained headway. As sparks from the burning roofs fell into the kegs of powder, terrific explosions followed, hurling flaming wood to the roofs of other houses. Gradually at first and then more rapidly the fire spread. As Armstrong later reported: "We were agreeably entertained with a quick succession of charged Guns gradually firing off as reached by the Fire, but much more with the vast explosion of sundry bags and large Cags of powder wherewith every house abounded."

As the fire reached the Jacobs house, he jumped out of a "cock-loft" window and was shot and killed in midair. A Pennsylvanian nearby scalped him. The Indians from beyond the river tried to cross to get into the conflict but were headed off by Armstrong's men. They kept up a sniping fire across the river all through the battle.

Now, from one of the burning houses came a woman, crying in English that she was white. The Pennsylvanians, fearing a ruse, watched her warily until they noted she was followed by several children of Caucasian features. Then the woman and her children were received on the Pennsylvanian side of the battle line. All told there came from the burning huts two white women, one man, one boy, and seven girls. One was a

Virginian. The others had been stolen from various Pennsylvania settlements.

Armstrong estimated they had killed 30 or 40 Indians. Of this he was not certain as some bodies were consumed in the burning houses. Some of the wounded were drowned while trying to swim the river. Other wounded crawled into the corn patches where they may have died.

The village destroyed, it was necessary to retreat before runners could summon reinforcements from Venango or Duquesne. And so the Pennsylvanians rounded up a few Delaware horses to carry the wounded, the women and the children, and marched away. Indians followed on the flanks, firing as chance offered, but with little success. The Pennsylvanians retreated from tree to tree, firing so effectively that the Indians desisted.

Back at the place where a detachment had been left to guard the horses, blankets, and haversacks, Armstrong found that the detail had been attacked by the 24 Delawares they had left undisturbed the night before. The attacking party had been beaten off, but not until the Indians had stampeded some of the pack horses.

All day the Pennsylvanians retreated. They came after sunset to the scaffold they had built. It was undisturbed, and they rested long enough to gobble food and were on their way by moonlight. In five days they were back in Fort Shirley, displaying scalps and Indian articles as proof of their victory.

Colonel Armstrong had the mournful duty of reporting to widows, children, and other relatives that he had lost 17 dead. Thirteen were wounded. To Governor Denny he wrote: "We must not despise the smallest Degree of success that God is pleased to give especially at a time of such general calamities."*

The Pennsylvania Assembly paid the men for their time, but

---

* Quotations from Armstrong and Captain Jacobs are from Armstrong's report in *Pennsylvania Archives,* Vol. II, first series, Philadelphia, 1852.

did nothing for the wounded, the widows, or orphans. The Philadelphia council voted £150 for the double purpose of relief for the distressed and a few medals for the officers. The medal awarded to Armstrong bore on its reverse side the coat of arms of Philadelphia and on its face a device of an officer followed by two soldiers, the officer pointing to a soldier shooting from behind a tree with an Indian prostrate before him. Beyond were log houses in flames. The legend read: "Kittanning destroyed by Col. Armstrong."

Today we remember Armstrong by the map. Present-day Kittanning is the seat of a county appropriately named Armstrong.

XX. *A Summer of Heartbreak*

ARMSTRONG'S exploit made him a hero from the hemlocks of the Kennebeck to the sedges of the Savannah, but his renown rested on this one feat alone. Out of New Hampshire came a paladin of such incredulous courage and stamina that his hundred hit-and-run victories or defeats — a new one every few weeks — placed his name on every tongue month after month.

The luster of the reputation of Robert Rogers has endured even to our own time as the theme of song and verse and drama. At the age of eight he already was winning fame in New Hampshire as a frontier hunter. By the time he was 14 he was a soldier in King George's War. In the interval of peace he won a rather dubious reputation as a smuggler, carrying New England goods through the wilderness to Canada and Canadian goods back to New England, outwitting the customs officers of both King Louis and King George, learning to speak French and several Indian tongues, and becoming as well acquainted with wilderness ways as a doe learns to know her fawn.

In 1755, just turned 24, he became adept at making and passing counterfeit currency. Officers were about to arrest him, when he hastened to join the army of William Johnson on Lake George, and became the captain of Rogers' Rangers. His zest for danger, his physical superiority, his friendliness, and his good humor when wet and cold and hungry won the affection of every soldier. Both friend and foe recognized him at sight because of his big, broad nose. His first lieutenant was a man like him, John Stark, who became an American general in the Revolution.

Again and again Rogers' Rangers scouted Fort Ticonderoga, fighting like Indians, attacking small details and scattering in all directions upon encountering superior forces. Each day Rogers fixed a rendezvous for the coming night as a rallying point in case they became separated. If scattered, each man had to rely on his own speed and resourcefulness to survive and reach the rendezvous. Some did not survive, but it was thought better for a few to die than for all of the rangers to be destroyed.

In January, 1757, they skated from Fort William Henry northward across Lake George to the narrows where Lake George joins Lake Champlain. The night was so frigid that the air they breathed would bite the lungs of any not inured to arctic climes. These men had no tents and only one blanket each. They found a snowdrift, scooped out a hole, lay boughs on the bottom of the hole, and snuggled together to sleep warm. For breakfast they ate dried beef, each man carrying his own rations. When their supply was gone, they would survive by hunting.

Past Ticonderoga they skated and came to Crown Point. There they burned the Frenchmen's barns containing food for men and horses. Back they came to Ticonderoga on a night so cold frost rimmed their brows and eyelashes. They killed several of the sentries, took prisoners, and drove off cattle, which they, on skates, herded back to Fort William Henry.

In summer they traveled by boat, hid the boats in the woods, sneaked past the outposts to the wharves of Ticonderoga to sink cargo boats newly arrived from Montreal and not yet unloaded. Cunning and sly, they were a constant menace to the enemy and felt themselves rewarded by an occasional supply of food they captured from the French on which they gorged themselves.

One winter day as the wind moaned in the treetops they were lurking in a thicket beside the lake between Crown Point and Ticonderoga when they saw passing by a few sleds driven by Canadian teamsters. Out sallied Rogers with 74 rangers on snowshoes. The enemy was so inconsequential it seemed a simple thing to surround and capture them.

Just then 300 Frenchmen hove in sight around a headland and in an instant took six rangers prisoner. There was nothing to do but scatter, but they left 14 of their number sprawled rigid on the ice. Rogers himself was shot in the head, and others were wounded, but each was left to care for himself. Any man who failed to make it to the rendezvous was out of luck.

Rogers was anxious as he made his way to the rendezvous. There he took time to scratch the bullet from his skull and convince himself that he would survive. But what of the rest? Silently Rogers counted the men as they arrived one by one. He hoped his loss would not be too great. Counting himself, 55 came in. All had been saved except the six prisoners and the 14 on the ice.

Then, to his astonishment, a fifty-sixth appeared. This extra man was Sergeant Joshua Martin, one of the 14 left for dead. When the French kicked him to make sure he was dead, he had regained consciousness but lay still until the enemy had gone. Then he hobbled to the rendezvous, recovered from his wounds, and lived to a good old age.

While Rogers was winning glory in his raid against the French, Loudon gained a laurel wreath by beating the people of the colonies. In the fall of 1756 he ordered the British regulars to be quartered at the expense of the people of Boston, New York, and Philadelphia. Boston accepted the burden,

Philadelphia yielded only after Loudon threatened, and New York grudgingly agreed to quarter the enlisted men but required the officers to pay. Loudon sent an order that officers also should be quartered at the expense of the inhabitants. When the mayor called on him to argue, his lordship yelled: "Billet my officers upon free quarters this day. If you do not, I'll order here all the troops in North America."

The mayor yielded. The colonial troops were no problem. They went to their homes for winter quarters. Loudon left 400 men to garrison Fort William Henry and Fort Edward. The garrisons were mostly British regulars together with Rogers' Rangers.

Having disposed of his men, Loudon called a conference of governors to announce his grand design for 1757. They met at Philadelphia, where Washington attended so that he could press on Loudon the importance of taking and holding Fort Duquesne. He and Dinwiddie argued that raids like those of Armstrong and Rogers were great morale builders but did not win the war. If the Indian incursions on Pennsylvania, Maryland, and Virginia were to be stopped, it was necessary to take and hold Fort Duquesne.

Loudon listened but did not agree. He informed the governors that the three colonies had to contrive their own defense through 1757. He was going to take Quebec, not by advancing by way of Ticonderoga, where he would be subjected to forest fighting and ambuscades. He would go by sea. First he would take Louisburg, a city on Cape Breton Island with a large land-locked harbor where a French fleet lay. The island abutted the Gulf of St. Lawrence, the approach most likely to be used by a British fleet attempting to enter the St. Lawrence River, the water roadway to Quebec.

One concession Washington did gain. Loudon relieved the Virginia troops from holding Fort Cumberland and assigned

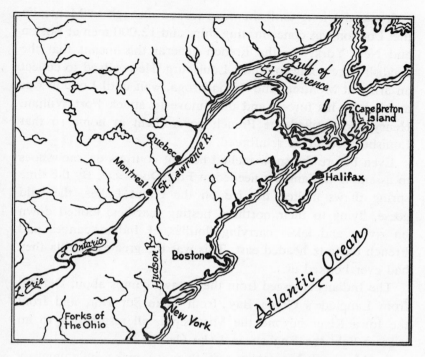

How Cape Breton Island guards Quebec

them to Maryland. Governor Sharpe, elevating Dagworthy to the rank of colonel, sent him to Cumberland with two companies.

In command of the colonial forces from Pennsylvania south, Loudon named a king's officer, Colonel John Stanwix, who was present at the conference. Washington and his new superior officer became friendly associates. Stanwix established headquarters at Carlisle, from which he took charge of the defense of Pennsylvania, leaving Washington a free hand in Virginia.

It was not long until the news leaked through to Montcalm that Loudon was concentrating ships and 12,000 men at Boston and New York. To the French general this meant that the English were going to attack Louisburg. He resolved to collect an army at Montreal and Ticonderoga, wait until Loudon was at sea with his forces, and then move to attack Fort William Henry. He notified the French government at home so that Louisburg could be reinforced.

Even before the snow melted he sent couriers on snowshoes to assemble Indians not needed at Fort Duquesne. By the time spring thaws melted the ice on the Great Lakes, the wild geese, flying to their northern nesting marshes, looked down on rivers and lakes carrying flotillas of Indian canoes and French bateaux headed east. This was the greatest flotilla they had ever honked at.

The Indians emerged from the Ottawa camps about Detroit, from Langlade's Green Bay, from Lake Superior, and from the Iowa River beyond the Mississippi, all responding to an urge to fight the English on Lake George.

At Montreal Montcalm met them to make inflammatory speeches and to war-sing with them. This conqueror of Oswego fascinated them and they him. In letters to his wife he lamented their lack of chivalry in dealing with prisoners, but he agreed with one of his officers, who wrote to his home in France: "We can no more do without them than without cavalry on the plain."

Months were lost as Montcalm waited for Loudon to embark for Louisburg. In the meantime the Indians skulked beside the trail between Fort Edward and Fort William Henry, matching Rogers' Rangers with feats of daring deviltry. Once at Fort Edward they drove in the pickets and came back to Ticonderoga with 32 scalps.

By midsummer Loudon set sail for Halifax, the jumping off

place for an attack on Louisburg. The time had come for Montcalm to strike and it came none too soon. Food was running out. Montcalm had to provision 6000 French regulars and Canadians besides 2000 Indians. With so many hearty eaters and with Rogers raiding the supply lines it was difficult to bring enough food from Montreal. At the same time, game was disappearing and they could not seine enough fish for so many people.

The general was glad when on August 1 he could move toward Fort William Henry, which was defended by 2200 men supported by 1600 more at Fort Edward. He mounted cannon about the fort, and soon the enlisted men at Fort Edward, hearing the booming of guns, begged to be led into the fight, but their cautious commander, knowing the numbers of the enemy, felt it more prudent to remain where they were.

While solid shot and explosives battered the wooden bastions of Fort William Henry, three hundred defenders died of shot and shell and under crashing timbers. What was worse, the hospital was filled with men ill of smallpox. Some rose from bed to fight until they dropped in their places. Lieutenant Colonel Monro, the commander, finally raised a white flag, and Montcalm received his surrender. Since he had no food for the prisoners, the French general directed Monro's men to be ready to march to Fort Edward the following day.

But before the vanquished marched out, Montcalm called the Indian chiefs together and secured their solemn pledges to keep their men from attacking the prisoners. He further instructed Monro to knock in the heads of the rum casks so that the Indians would not become drunk and unmanageable.

In the late afternoon Monro's men moved to an entrenched camp where they were to spend the night. Instantly the Indians swarmed over the parapets of the vacated fort to massacre the sick and scalp them. They even followed the English to their camp and attacked them there, but Montcalm persuaded them to cease.

At daybreak as the English began their march to Fort Edward, the Indians plundered their baggage and began killing them for their uniforms and scalps. Montcalm ran among them greatly distressed. He begged the Indians to kill him, but spare the prisoners. They yielded to his pleas after killing about 50 men and carrying off 200 prisoners for torture or adoption. Some of the Indians, disappointed in their failure to take scalps, dug up those who had died of smallpox and retrieved their scalps. To protect Monro's men, the French regulars escorted the prisoners to Fort Edward and freed them there.

Montcalm wanted to take Fort Edward, too, and was criticized by Vaudreuil for his failure, but he was almost entirely out of food. Further, Vaudreuil had promised the Canadian militiamen that they could return home in time for the late August harvest. The Indians, too, were making off with their scalps and trophies to boast of their deeds and dance the victory dance before the admiring girls in their home villages. The general, therefore, contented himself with taking off such military stores as his bateaux could carry. The rest he burned along with the fort.

The Indians, when they arrived at Montreal, were met by Vaudreuil, who ransomed the English prisoners who had not already been tortured to death.

Montcalm's victory cost his Indian allies dearly. The germs of smallpox, with which they were infected at Fort William Henry, incubated while they were on their way home. Since no Indian had ever had smallpox until the disease was brought to America by the white people, the red men had no immunity to it, and they were subject to greater virulence than white people. Knowing nothing of contagion, the Indians took no precautions for isolating the sick. From village to village the

germs were carried, spreading to tribes that never had participated in the war. A war chief, watching all of his sons die,
wept: "If I could only see the enemy who fights me, I could
protect my home."

Perhaps Loudon would have thought the loss of Fort William
Henry well worth its cost if he could have taken Louisburg.
He sent fast sailing vessels from Halifax to scout the city and
its defenses. Soon they returned to report that three French
fleets instead of one were anchored in the harbor. Troops in
great numbers manned the bastions. It was evident that an
attack would be folly. And so Loudon returned with his army
to winter quarters in Boston, New York, and Philadelphia.

The Americans regarded Loudon's efforts with heartbreak
and disgust. They discussed with each other the incompetence
of the king's commanders, not one of whom had won a victory.
They measured them alongside Rogers, Bradstreet, Johnson,
Armstrong, and Washington. They concluded that in case of
war between the British and the Americans, the Americans
could win. That was a dangerous thought. Some day they
would dare to try their theory and overthrow the king's rule.
But first they had to defeat the French and Indians.

XXI. *George Courts a Widow*

THE morale of the Virginia regiment ebbed to its very lowest when the news came of the loss of Fort William Henry and the failure to fight at Louisburg. At the same time it raised the spirit of the Ohio Indians. Since they had not participated in the reduction of William Henry, they became ambitious to reap honors by raids into Pennsylvania, Maryland, and Virginia.

Washington, in reviewing the last two years of defensive effort, reported that he had lost 100 men killed in 20 skirmishes in 1756 and 1757 promised a similar record. In a letter to Loudon he excused his men for deserting. He showed that no provision was made for anyone incapacitated in battle. He was discharged, dropped from the colonial payroll, and left to live on relatives or beg from strangers. "They thought themselves bubbled," wrote Washington. "This caused desertion; and the deserters, spreading over the country, recounted their sufferings and want of pay, which rags and poverty sufficiently testified, fixed in the minds of the populace such horrid impressions of the hardships they had encountered, that no arguments could remove these prejudices, or facilitate recruiting service."

Washington recalled that in June, 1756, a committee of the House of Burgesses visited the troops at the front. The committeemen promised to provide winter clothing by October. It failed to arrive all winter long. Men shivered in summer garb or bought clothing with their meager pay. "I have seen a soldier," reported Washington, "go upon command with a new pair of shoes, which perhaps cost him from seven shillings six pence to ten shillings and return without any; so much do they wear in wading creeks, fording rivers and clambering mountains covered with rocks."

Washington tried to stop desertions by calling a court martial, which condemned three men to death. One had deserted three times and the other two had been definitely insubordinate in ways other than desertion. The colonel paraded the troops to witness the hanging, hoping thereby to instill respect through fear. The men, standing in close ranks, sulkily watched as the three culprits swung from their gibbets. That night sixteen deserted.

In an attempt to curb profanity, Washington directed punishment by 25 lashes. The miscreants groaned under the lashings and cursed again. In an attempt to get rid of tippling houses so that he could restrict his men to the ration of one gill of rum a day, Washington became a candidate for the House of Burgesses, announcing that he would strive for a bill to prohibit sales of liquor to soldiers. The tippling houses entered a candidate of their own and won over the colonel.

He thought to try religion and read from Scripture and the prayer book at the head of his command. The men listened, but their mood continued to be bent on sin. A chaplain, he hoped, would do the trick. Braddock had had a chaplain, but the Virginia clergy turned a deaf ear to Dinwiddie's plea for volunteers.

In hot anger the governor wrote the Lord Bishop of London, railing on the worthlessness of the Virginia clergy. He related that some of the reverend professors at William and Mary College had been so drunk they set a bad example to the students. He alleged that the minister of Hamilton Parish was guilty of drunkenness and almost every vice except murder. He almost was guilty of murder too, so Dinwiddie related, for he tied his wife by her legs to a bedpost and cut her with a knife until she was near death.

Washington had always placed a high value on the ability of the Indians to serve as scouts. In 1757 the allies he desired joined him. They were Catawabas and Cherokees, who hated the Ohio Indians. They expected presents, of course, but the Burgesses voted insufficient money for presents.

Edward Aiken of South Carolina asked Loudon to make him superintendent of Indian affairs for the southern colonies so that he could relieve Washington of dealing with the Indians. Aiken was a member of the governor's council of his colony. He had negotiated treaties with the Indians and rated himself an expert in dealing with them, but he was not expert enough to keep them content without presents. Gradually most of the red men drifted home. Washington implored Loudon to name Gist as superintendent of Indian affairs. The best Loudon did was to name Gist as an assistant to Aiken.

While most of the Indians went away, a few remained to fight for Washington with élan. Washington usually detailed an officer or a few soldiers to go with scouting parties of Indians. Some were cut off in the woods and slaughtered. Others ventured to within a warwhoop of Fort Duquesne to bring home French and Indian scalps, for which bounties were paid by Dinwiddie. Their raids were always touch and go.

For example, the details have been recorded of a sortie by 15 Cherokees accompanied by five soldiers, including Lieutenant James Baker. They were on the headwaters of Turtle Creek about 20 miles from Fort Duquesne, the white men all naked to the waist like the Indians, when they ran into a party of three French officers and ten enlisted men. The Frenchmen, supposing that these seminaked people were their own Indians, watched them passively as they approached. They were at close musket range when Baker gave the quiet order to fire.

Three Frenchmen fell dead and two wounded. One was seized and captured. This left seven unhit or slightly wounded, who ran. In the melee one of the Cherokees, Swallow Warrior, was killed. His son, trying to help him, was shot through both thighs.

Since the forest was swarming with other parties of the enemy, prudence dictated that the son of Swallow Warrior, who could not walk, should be abandoned. The Cherokees killed the two wounded Frenchmen, ripped off the five scalps, and made off. One of the Virginia soldiers, however, picked up the wounded Cherokee by the hands and carried him pickaback.

The soldier ran with his burden after the retreating raiders until he was too exhausted to run longer. Then another of the white men relieved him. By relays the five white soldiers carried the wounded Indian all the way to Fort Cumberland, reaching it four days later, having subsisted on wild onions. They dared not take time to hunt for game, for they knew the seven Frenchmen who had escaped would be sure to organize a party for retribution. At Cumberland they rested a few days and then returned to Fort Loudon. The chivalry of the white men in carrying the wounded Indian helped cement the friendship of the Cherokees.

The presence of Washington's Indians and white rangers in the forest between Fort Loudon and Fort Duquesne reduced the attacks on the settlements, but it stirred desire for revenge. Indians hung around Fort Loudon and Winchester to kill and scalp when they could.

It may be that the French officers at Duquesne offered a high bounty for the scalp of Lord Fairfax. At least his lordship realized that his scalp would be a handsome prize. He, therefore, gave directions that his most valued possessions be packed so that he could retreat to Belvoir. Washington learned of this and raised emphatic protest. If Fairfax fled, it would set a bad example to the settlers. And so he remained, risking his noble scalp for the good of the cause. Despite his lordship's example the frontier was so consumed with anxiety and terror that Washington wrote to Speaker Robison: "If we pursue a defensive plan next campaign, there will not by autumn be one living soul on this side of the Blue Ridge."

In October dysentery had Washington in its grip again. He wrote of it to Dinwiddie, and the governor commanded him to remain at his post. It was well that winter was coming with snows to give the Indian raiders pause, for in late November Washington was almost prostrate. He could scarcely sit his horse until he reached Mount Vernon, where he reeled from the saddle and took to his bed. For the next four months he was often in agony. Sometimes he was well enough to ride to nearby places, but mostly he lounged in front of the fireplace or kept to his bed.

For that matter, Dinwiddie became ill too. He petitioned the king to relieve him, and sailed home with his wife and daughters. There Rebecca grew to womanhood and married. Elizabeth died a spinster. We cannot help believing that she thought often with fondness of the bashful, pockmarked Virginia colonel, whose name grew radiant with honor through the years.

Washington could not help lamenting that the British high command was bungling the war, but in the British Isles they lamented too. Lord Chesterfield mourned, "We are no longer a nation." Members of Parliament and others of influence demanded that William Pitt be called to head the government. Even the king's own son, the Duke of Cumberland, joined with those who wanted Pitt. Very few people liked him. The king hated him. He added nothing to his popularity by asserting: "I am sure I can save this country, and that nobody else can."

Those supporting him forgave his conceit, for they believed

he was telling the truth. The king, yielding to pressure, formed a coalition government headed by Pitt, who was given exclusive control of military and foreign affairs. Pitt resolved to reduce France to the rating of the second power in the world. He sent more men and money to help Frederick the Great, whose troops were outnumbered five to one. In India he supported Clive, who wrecked French dominion there and made India a vassal state of the British Empire for almost two centuries.

As for the war in the colonies, Pitt set out to destroy France in America. Four times, commencing with 1689, France and England had fought merciless war in America in which Indians were engaged on both sides. This fourth war was to be the last if Pitt had his way.

To accomplish this last task he needed generals and he began scouting for them. He assigned Jeffrey Amherst, who had fought with credit in Germany, to take Louisburg and clear the way for a sea attack on Quebec.

Next he jerked Loudon, and he would have removed Abercromby, too, but Pitt had to keep in mind that his party had no majority in Parliament. He was but the head of a coalition government, merely accepted by the opposition majority in Parliament. Abercromby had many friends who argued that Loudon and not Abercromby was responsible for bungling of the last two years. Pitt, therefore, thought to get rid of Abercromby by making him the over-all commander, a position to which his rank entitled him. All orders, however, came from Pitt and Abercromby merely had a desk job of passing the orders on.

For the Ticonderoga effort, Pitt dispatched to America George Augustus Howe, a British lord accustomed to luxury at home. He joined Rogers' Rangers in December of 1757 to learn the art of wilderness fighting at the side of a master. He washed his own clothing in ice water. He turned meat over the fire so that he might eat. He fought in desperate combats. With Rogers at his side he ranged the forest until he was thoroughly familiar with the terrain and had looked down into Ticonderoga and Crown Point. News of what he was doing spread through New England and New York all winter long. By spring he was heading an army of devoted volunteers who trusted and loved him.

Pitt did not overlook Fort Duquesne. He directed Abercromby to assign to that campaign Colonel John Forbes, whom Pitt promoted to the rank of brigadier general. Forbes had never exercised high command, but as a line officer he had shown bravery and initiative in the War of Austrian Succession and had come to America early in 1757 as colonel of a regiment. He went with Loudon on the Louisburg campaign, which ended at Halifax without a battle. Loudon had recognized the ability of Forbes and made him adjutant general, in which capacity he gained executive experience. Pitt believed that Forbes had the makings of an army leader.

News that Pitt was planning to send an army to take and hold Fort Duquesne both elated and depressed Washington. He was elated because he believed the taking of Fort Duquesne would end the hopeless defensive warfare. He was depressed because he feared he would not be well enough to have a part in the great adventure.

In late March he was still weak from illness, but he called for his horse and rode to Williamsburg to confer with officers of the colony. He also went to see a physician, who told him that he was free of dysentery and that outdoor exercise would quickly restore his strength.

He resolved to return to his command at Winchester, for spring raids would soon begin and he was needed there. As he rode out of Williamsburg it was supposed by everybody that he would take the direct road to his post of duty, but he did a strange thing. After he had gone a few miles, he came to a fork in the dirt road. Instead of pursuing the direct route to Winchester, he drew on his horse's right rein, came to the Pamunkey River, crossed it by the ferry, and rode to the White House plantation, the home of a widow, Martha Custis, and her two children. Her husband, Daniel Parke Custis, had died the year before. Martha was administrator of his 21,000-acre estate as well as other important assets. It is presumed that she had received several offers of marriage, as it was not customary for a woman as rich as Martha to remain a widow long in colonial Virginia. It may be recalled that Lawrence Washington's widow mourned only five months before she remarried.

Washington's account book shows that when he left for Winchester he gave 30 shillings as gratuities to Martha's slaves who cared for his horse and performed other services during his visit. Perhaps he knew that it was well to have the slaves on his side. A few weeks later he again felt it was important that he consult in person with the authorities at Williamsburg. After concluding his business, he again rode home by way of the White House and again left 30 shillings in tips.

A month later he was back in Williamsburg. He probably could have cared for his military affairs by correspondence, but there were matters at the White House that could be handled only by a personal call.

As he arrived this time all nature was atune with the song in his heart. The doctor had been right. His health was perfect. He was feeling as fit as any 26-year-old man ought to feel. He was just a few months older than Martha, who let him know by the shine in her eyes that she was glad to see him again.

It was the end of May when mockingbirds are nesting, when they rise straight up on beating pinions and almost split their throats as they voice their happiness to the world. It was the time when they sing all day and all moonlit nights, when they even awaken in the small hours in the dark of the moon to warble the sweetest music ever heard on earth and warble it with such intensity they rouse the other birds of the Pamunkey woodlands to respond with a rapturous chorus. Though the windows were shut to keep out the night air, the sweet notes trilled down the wide chimneys and out of the fireplaces into the rooms of the White House.

How could Martha say no in a time like that? She said yes, but George's stay must have been brief, for his books show that his tips totaled only 12 shillings, sixpence.

It would have been pleasanter to resign his command and remain at the White House. Martha not only was rich, she was good to look at, and her two children, ages 4 and 2, were well behaved. But Washington had a job of work. Virginia was looking to him to end the war he had started. He had to go where great deeds waited, where men would suffer and die.

A slave brought his horse to the block and he rode into the West.

XXII. *Vamping Up the Big Stroke*

NEWS that Pitt was preparing a big stroke to knock Fort Duquesne out of the war stirred up Virginia. The Burgesses, no longer niggardly, voted to enroll and maintain two regiments of 1000 men each.

The First Regiment under Washington needed only to be recruited to full strength. The Second Regiment had to start from scratch, and so it was voted that those enlisting in the Second need serve only until December 1. Some classes of recruits in the Second were given more pay than the same classes in the First. All recruits in either regiment were paid a bounty of ten pounds.

All of this angered Washington, whose veterans, some with as much as three years of service, received no bounties. To John Blair, president of the Virginia Council, who was acting governor until a successor to Dinwiddie should arrive, Washington remonstrated: "The soldiers of the first regiment think their claim upon the country equally good, if not better than that of the second."

Washington's protest had no effect. There was nothing Blair could do about it, for the Burgesses had passed the law and had gone home. Because of his longer service, Washington was designated as commander of both regiments when the two should be brigaded together. He would perform the duties of brigadier general, but his rank would remain that of colonel, the highest rank that could be conferred without a king's commission.

Commander of the Second Regiment was William Byrd, three years older than Washington, who had an English education and, after schooling, remained in England to study drill and maneuver under British tacticians. He was of a family of planters that had long been prominent in the councils of the colony, and is still prominent after two centuries.

Byrd had served his colony on missions to the Cherokees and Catawabas and in 1757 had been an officer under Loudon in the ill-starred Louisburg campaign. While Loudon's army was idle at Halifax, waiting for the big push that never came, Byrd made the acquaintance of Forbes, who learned to regard him highly and doubtless would have preferred him as ranking officer of the Virginians rather than Washington, whom he had never met. Washington had been handicapped through four years by the necessity of selling himself to his superiors, who kept changing.

First he met the doubts of Dinwiddie and the council. Then he served under Fry, Innes, Braddock, Shirley, Loudon, Stanwix, and now Forbes. Hoping to acquaint Forbes with the fact that the ranking Virginia soldier existed, he wrote the general when he came to take his command at Philadelphia early in April. "It gives me no small pleasure," he began, "that an Officer of your experience, abilities, and good Character, should be appointed to command the Expedition, and it is with equal satisfaction I congratulate you upon the promising appearance of a glorious campaign."

To Stanwix, who had been promoted to brigadier general and placed in charge of the central New York district, Washington penned a letter of congratulation and asked Stanwix to put in a good word with Forbes. There was still another man who might gain the general's ear. That was Major Francis Halkett, whose father and brother were slain at the Battle of the Monongahela. It will be recalled that Francis was a comrade of Washington on that expedition. He was now back in America as secretary to General Forbes. "I really feel a degree of satisfaction upon the prospect of meeting you again," Washington wrote Halkett.

Washington had hoped that, because of his experience, he might be placed second in command under Forbes. This was not to be. Pitt already had his eye on Colonel Henry Bouquet. This 39-year-old Swiss soldier of fortune had been a fighting man for 20 years, serving in the armies of Switzerland, Sardinia, and the Netherlands. In 1756 he was offered higher pay and higher rank by the British government and again changed his allegiance. For a time he had been stationed in South Carolina. Pitt transferred him to Philadelphia to be the right hand man under Forbes.

Forbes for a time detailed Bouquet to recruiting service in Pennsylvania, later dispatching him to the frontier to build a road and to erect forts at intervals beside it. Forbes studied the Braddock campaign and was determined to learn all he could from it. Besides Halkett, he had in his command Sir John St. Clair, who had cut the road for Braddock and was now with Forbes as a major in charge of the commissary.

One thing brought Washington unbounded satisfaction. In letters to the governors and in instructions to his commanders in various fronts, Pitt directed that officers commissioned by the colonial governors were to have equal rank with those who had a king's commission. No longer could a king's captain claim to outrank a colonial colonel.

Through April and May the line officers under Washington and Byrd carried on an aggressive campaign to fill their regiments. This was a difficult task, for the population of Virginia was but 125,000, of whom almost one half were slaves. The plantation owners were not expected to enlist as common soldiers, for someone had to remain on the land to keep the slaves in hand. Of course, it was unthinkable that slaves should bear arms. The small farmers could not be spared from their fields in the summer. It was all they could do, since tillage and harvest were by hand labor, to grow food enough to maintain their families.

Recruits, therefore, had to be found among single men with few responsibilities. The recruiting officers appealed to self-interest and patriotism. First, they exploited the fact that unless Fort Duquesne were reduced, Virginia's frontier would be pushed back to tide water and perhaps into the sea. If the single men wanted to survive and wanted their relatives to survive, they had to fight.

Of course, the bounty of ten pounds in a lump sum was a big inducement. Few Virginians had ever owned that much all in one piece. Further, the land in Virginia was mostly in big holdings. A poor man could acquire a farm only by leasing it from Lord Fairfax or some other big landowner. But drive out the French and the Ohio land was there for the taking.

Then there was the glory of it. The war was the biggest thing in the memory of any living Virginian. Those who helped win it would be honored all their days. Those single men who failed to volunteer would forever after need to explain why. The Second Regiment offered the added inducement that its men needed to serve only until December 1. Washington's officers countered this by showing that as soon as Fort Duquesne was taken, the war would be over and all would be discharged. Everybody was sure the war would be over before autumn. Then, too, why not fight under Virginia's proved hero?

The recruiting was almost complete when early in June Francis Fauquier, the new lieutenant governor, arrived from England. Like Dinwiddie, he performed all the duties of governor, while his superior remained in England. Washington knew he had to begin at once to sell himself to the new governor. From his headquarters at Fort Loudon, he wrote: "Hon'ble Sir: Although but a poor hand at Complimenting, but permit me, nevertheless to offer your Hon'r my congratulations on your appointment; and safe arrival to a Government which His Majesty has been Graciously pleas'd to entrust you with the Administration of, and to assure you, that I most sincerely wish your Administration may be attended with pleasure to yourself and strength to the People Governed."

At about that time Bouquet inspected the troops raised by Washington and Byrd. It was the first time the Virginians had met their immediate superior. They found him easy to deal with, and he, on his part, learned from them.

One of the first problems they had to settle was that of a uniform. During Braddock's campaign an attempt had been made to dress the Virginians in blue woolen uniforms. Unfortunately there were not in all America a sufficient number of blue uniforms to clothe one regiment, let alone two. But there was an abundance of hunting shirts. Washington recommended this type of frontier dress for both Virginia regiments to be worn not only by the men, but by the officers, including the colonels. Half apologizing, Washington explained to Bouquet: "Nothing but the uncertainty of it taking with the General causes me to hesitate a moment . . . and proceeding as light as any Indian in the Woods. 'Tis an unbecoming dress, I confess, for an officer; but convenience rather than shew, I think should be consulted."

Washington rigged up two companies in his recommended uniforms under command of Major Lewis and sent them to Bouquet for inspection. Bouquet approved the uniforms instantly and asked Forbes to add his approval. Only a short time previous Forbes had written to Bouquet that they must learn from enemy Indians and from provincials.

Here was a case in point. Summers are hot in America. Why

burden the men with uniforms for show? Forbes gave his assent to the new garb, and soon the two regiments were in picturesque frontier uniforms with shirts outside their breeches and with leggings to the knees. A tough looking lot they were with faith in their aim, and woe betide the Frenchman who lingered to look upon them askance.

With his men accoutered Washington was ready for the big stroke. The year before, in discussing man power with Stanwix, Washington had estimated that he could take Duquesne with 3000 men. Now, as he saw it, all Forbes need do was to issue the command to march. But the weeks passed, and the two Virginia regiments loitered at Winchester.

XXIII. *Keeping His Neck In*

AS IT appeared to Washington and Byrd, Forbes moved like a turtle with his neck in the shell. In early April he established headquarters at Philadelphia and was soon joined by his own regiment of Scottish Highlanders. A Scotchman himself, he thought no one else could fight like a kilted Scot. His regiment of 1400 was the apple of his eye and he designed it as the spearhead of his army.

His closest advisers were his secretary, Halkett, and Major James Grant, a Highlander. For a time he also placed great stock in Sir John St. Clair, for this British officer, as well as Halkett, had been at the Battle of the Monongahela. Forbes wanted to know where Braddock erred so that he would not make the same mistakes, and to St. Clair and Halkett he turned for information on Braddock's errors.

For one thing, Braddock had no forts west of Cumberland to which he might fall back in case of reverse. Forbes, therefore, instructed Bouquet to build forts at intervals and ordered St. Clair, who was chief commissary officer, to store provisions there for men and horses.

Halkett and St. Clair remembered vividly that Braddock had been routed by French and Indians hidden by foliage. Forbes inquired of Philadelphia traders and learned that the region through which he would pass was to a great extent forested by deciduous trees, vines, and undergrowth, and that the trees shed their leaves in late October. Very well, he would get into position to reach Fort Duquesne about November 1.

At no time did Forbes notify Washington that his men were to remain in camp all summer. From a year's residence in America, he had learned that the people of the colonies were willful and quick to start an argument. Never in his 48 years had he encountered such people. His adult life had been spent in the army where he had been schooled to unquestioning obedience to his superiors and had expected unquestioning obedience from his inferiors. The contrary Americans would ask why, and if they were given a reason would argue. The truth is that if he had told Washington he did not intend to reach Fort Duquesne before November 1, the Virginia colonel would have presented a mouthful of back talk.

Forbes had been in Philadelphia only a short time when an urgent dispatch from Washington reported 700 Cherokees and Catawabas encamped at Winchester and eager to fight. These red allies were especially skilled in stealthy forest warfare and needed attention as Forbes was quick to recognize. But Washington had no rations and no presents for them. What was more, the king's government had denoted Sir William Johnson as superintendent of Indian affairs with Edward Aiken as his deputy in charge of the southern Indians. Washington had been cautioned not to interfere.

Forbes immediately sent presents, ammunition, and food for the Indians. He appealed first to Johnson and then to Aiken for help, and both, instead of obeying, sent excuses. They had other duties. This exasperated Forbes, and he became more exasperated when dysentery sent him to bed, from which he directed the building of his army.

Since Pennsylvania was the most populous of the thirteen colonies, Forbes expected it to contribute more soldiers than Virginia. This was possible despite the fact that a large segment of the population of 220,000 was made up of pacifists, for the Pennsylvania people had few slaves. Of course, first Pennsylvania rank went to Colonel Armstrong, hero of Kittanning. Subordinate officers were Colonel James Burd, not to be confused with Colonel Byrd of Virginia, and Lieutenant Colonel Hugh Mercer, unrelated to Virginia's George Mercer. These officers enlisted 2700 volunteers, who were raised under a provision of the Pennsylvania legislature that their term of enlistment would end on December 1, the same as Byrd's Second Virginia. Of course, the colonial governments had no knowledge of Forbes' plan not to strike Duquesne until after the leaves fell. The Pennsylvanians were dressed in summer shirts the same as the Virginians. There were also 300 Pennsylvanians enrolled in the Royal Americans, clad in coats as bright as cherries in June and officered by British martinets. These men enlisted for the duration of the war and were designed as the elite of the provincials.

With 3000 Pennsylvanians, 1400 Highlanders, 950 Virginians under Washington and 900 under Byrd, 150 each from Maryland and North Carolina and 100 from Delaware, Forbes had an army of 6500 men, not counting 1000 wagoners from various colonies, who carried arms and would help in a pinch. In addition Byrd had 65 Catawabas. The 700 Cherokees and Catawabas with Washington began to drift away because of neglect. By the end of summer all were gone.

With part of the army Bouquet started cutting a road west. As he advanced he requisitioned more men to garrison forts and to form a defensive screen for his axmen. He took the traveled road from Philadelphia to Carlisle and improved the existing road from Carlisle to Raystown, now Bedford, Pennsylvania, which is 31 miles north and a little east of Cumberland.

Raystown was a small trading post founded by John Wray, who traded with the Indians of the Ohio. Armstrong had built a Pennsylvania fort there in 1757. Bouquet enlarged this, constructing hospitals, storehouses, barracks, and stables.

Upon orders from Bouquet, the two Virginia regiments marched from Winchester to Cumberland and made camp there adjoining the fort. Washington imagined that Bouquet would quickly join him at Cumberland and all would go together by Braddock's Road to Fort Duquesne. The road required only that brush and saplings grown up in the last three years be cleared. So certain was he that the big stroke was about to begin that he wrote Martha: "We have begun the march to the Ohio. . . . I embrace the opportunity to send a few words to one whose life is now inseparable from mine. Since the happy hour when we made our pledges to each other, my thoughts have been continually going to you as another Self. That an all-powerful Providence may keep us both in safety is the prayer of your ever faithful and affectionate friend."

Washington did not march, and he began to wonder why Bouquet directed him to send two companies of veterans under Major Lewis to Raystown. Later Bouquet asked for four more companies under Lieutenant Colonel Stephen. If Bouquet was planning to march by way of Cumberland, why was he drawing the Virginians away? Finally Washington wrote to Bouquet: "I pray your Interest, most Sincerely, with the General, to get my Regiment and myself Included in the Number. If there needs any arguments to obtain this favor, I hope, without vanity, I may be allow'd to say that from long Intimacy, and frequent Scouting in these Woods, my Men are well acquainted with all the Passes and difficulties, as any Troops that will be employ'd."

With the Virginia regiments gone from Winchester, the Ohio Indians redoubled their raids on the Virginia frontier, whose defense now was left to the militia. They also raided Pennsylvania and crossed the Delaware River to take scalps in New Jersey. They even lurked around the camp at Cumberland, killing any straggling soldier, cattle herder, or dispatch rider they might find alone or in small groups. In retaliation Forbes directed Bouquet to send raiding parties, whom he styled commandoes, to waylay stragglers around Fort Duquesne.

As Washington idled at Cumberland, he had time to think of other things. An election was to be held, and two Burgesses were to be chosen from Frederick County, of which Winchester is the county seat. Washington wrote to a friend there and offered his name as a candidate. He made no effort other than to direct his campaign manager to treat all the voters to liquor.

The voters must have become inebriated, for the other three candidates also provided liquor. Washington paid a bill for 28 gallons of rum, 50 gallons of rum punch, 34 gallons of wine, 46 gallons of beer, and two gallons of cider. This was consumed by only 346 voters. Of this number 309 voted for Washington and 45 for his opponent. Washington's running mate got 239 votes and his opponent 199.

It was gratifying to receive so handsome a vote from the people he had tried to defend for three years and among whom he had toiled as a surveyor. He sent a letter of thanks to his manager, in which he complained of the slowness of Forbes, commenting: "Backwardness appears in all things but the aproach of Winter; that joggs on apace."

The question as to whether a king's officer outranked a colonial officer of higher nominal rank came to the fore for the last time while Lieutenant Colonel Stephen was at Raystown. St. Clair, who was but a major, complained to Stephen that his troops were slovenly and insolent. He directed Stephen to discipline his men. At this Stephen snarled a retort. St. Clair waited until he caught Stephen away from his men and had him arrested. Forbes ordered Stephen released.

And now a new secret that Forbes had kept came out. From St. Clair and Halkett Forbes learned that in going by Braddock's Road, it was necessary to cross the Youghiogheny and the Monongahela. From Pennsylvania traders he learned that he could avoid both rivers by taking a road farther north, which traders had often followed. In fact, it was an old Delaware Indian trail, leading through the Delaware settlement of Loyalhanna west of Laurel Hill and on to Fort Duquesne. The Delawares had abandoned Loyalhanna, but the trace to it still existed and was known as Raystown Path from the fact that John Wray had followed it as he had traded with the Indians, first at Loyalhanna and later on the site of Pittsburgh and still later at Logstown. Today U. S. Highway 30 follows very nearly the old path from Bedford to Ligonier, on the site of Loyalhanna. Some of the detours the Indians took to avoid rough terrain have been eliminated where modern road machinery has bulldozed away the mountains and engineers have bridged ravines and rivers.

Bouquet had St. Clair, with a small commando escort, explore as far as Loyalhanna. He returned to place his stamp of approval on the route, although he later outraged Forbes by changing his mind, giving as his reason that Braddock's Road needed only the clearing of the brush that had grown up in three years. Knowing Bouquet did not intend to reach Duquesne until the leaves had fallen, Forbes was confident that he had time to hew a new road, a task that would keep the men busy.

Washington viewed the new road with alarm. Not only would it take longer to build because the grades along Raystown Path were steeper, but it would provide a route direct from Philadelphia to the Forks of the Ohio and strengthen the claim of Pennsylvania to a region that Virginia claimed. He enlisted Byrd to write letters of protest. He also stirred Fauquier and Robinson to raise objections. Byrd, since he knew Forbes, took it up directly with him. He said that his Indians

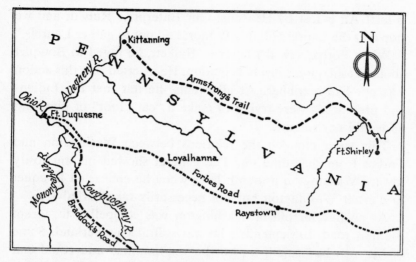

Forbes Road in relation to Braddock's Road and Armstrong's Trail

would not serve unless they could follow Braddock's Road. At this Forbes stormed, condemning a system of discipline by which the warrior told the general what to do. The scoundrels wouldn't run him, he asserted. But Forbes had a lot to learn about Indians. They took orders from nobody, not even their own chiefs, unless they wished to do so. They preferred the southern road as one less frequented by their enemies, the Shawnees and Delawares.

At Washington's insistence, he and Bouquet held a conference at Raystown. After the conference Washington, who apparently thought that the road by way of Loyalhanna was a design of Bouquet, appealed to Halkett to speak to Forbes. He referred to Braddock's Road as a beaten path "universally confess'd to be the best Passage through the Mountains" while the new road had still to be cut. Concluding, he burst out: "If Colo. Bouquet succeeds in this point with the General, all is lost! All is lost by Heavens! Our Enterprise Ruin'd; and we stop'd at the Laurel Hill this Winter; and not to gather Laurels."

When Forbes saw the letter to Halkett, he raged to Bouquet about Washington's insubordination. He asserted that this action was not like a soldier. At all events, he felt that the Indians and provincials were trying to make a "cat's foot" of him, and he would not submit.

This letter clouded the relations between Washington and Forbes from that time on. The general showed his animosity toward Washington a month later when he counseled Bouquet to consult Washington but not necessarily take his advice.

As an inferior officer Washington was compelled to accept the new road. In September he was still at Cumberland. Some of his men had smallpox, but he was immune and could call on them in the hospital without fear of contagion. To Speaker Robinson, he complained: "We are still Incamp'd here, very sickly; and quite dispirited at the prospect before Us. That appearance of Glory once in view, that hope, that laudable Ambition, is now no more! Tis dwindled into ease, Sloth, and fatal inactivity, and in a Word, All is lost."

XXIV. *Others in Action*

WHILE Washington was inactive, others were fighting. In June General Jeffrey Amherst landed on Cape Breton Island and took Louisburg. Among his subordinates was Edward Wolfe, the soul of the campaign, who took risks with the men, led the charges, and inspired victory. Pitt sent scouts to observe the operation, who returned with such glowing tributes of Wolfe that Pitt knew he had found a general. He directed Wolfe to return to England and organize a combined army and navy force to campaign against Quebec the following year.

Amherst was left for the time to garrison Louisburg, but he soon was needed at the Ticonderoga front. As has been related, Abercromby was over-all commander there and Lord Howe was placed at the head of 15,000 provincial troops, with only a few companies of regulars. Howe cut his hair short and ordered all his men to do likewise, so that the queues, the fashion at the time, would not become tangled in the brush. Instead of stockings, every man wore leggings to protect his legs from brambles. While advancing toward Ticonderoga, Howe was killed in the first engagement.

Abercromby took personal command. Opposing him were 3600 French and Canadians under Montcalm with only a few Indians. Smallpox had so reduced the number of warriors that the western Indians did not respond to the call for help. Montcalm's officers urged him to retreat, but he had studied Abercromby and mused: "Mayhap, he will fight for us."

Abercromby scouted Montcalm's position. The French had

thrown up an earthwork before Ticonderoga and faced this with an abatis of trees, felled with the brush side toward the enemy. Some of the stems of brush had been sharpened like spears. So dense was the abatis and so high was the earthwork that it would be difficult of passage for a man unopposed, let alone against an army of 3600. Abercromby could have by-passed the work and taken Ticonderoga from the rear. He had artillery with which he could have blasted the abatis away. Instead, he commanded a frontal charge. The Iroquois with him did not understand that sort of fighting. They drew aside and watched while the English charged seven times in six hours. They showed supreme courage and it is a remarkable fact that despite the handicap under which they were placed they killed or wounded 377 of the French. But they lost 1944 of their own before Abercromby realized that he had assigned a more difficult task than could be accomplished.

New England and New York mourned for their dead and muttered imprecations against "Mrs. Nabbycromby." The Iroquois went home disgusted. The Indians in the French interest told again the story of how Montcalm had trampled the English. Montcalm, himself, exulted: " 'Tis God the triumph wrought."

As Abercromby debated what to do next, Bradstreet came again with a plan he had proposed before, that of leading a commando raid on Fort Frontenac on the northeastern shore of Lake Ontario. Bradstreet now argued that it was necessary to win a victory, for the Iroquois were about ready to go in a body to join the French. His scouts brought the information that Fort Frontenac was poorly defended. Villiers, the commander, had been withdrawn to support Montcalm at Ticonderoga. The time to strike was before Villiers returned.

Bradstreet was so certain of victory that he offered to pay one half the cost of the expedition if he failed. This he was able to pay, for he was a merchant with ships on the sea. At length Abercromby yielded, but insisted that Bradstreet take not less than 2600 men. A few Oneidas joined Bradstreet as scouts. With this army he ascended the Mohawk River in boats to the carrying place, where he portaged to the Oswego and descended that river to its mouth. There on the ruins of the fort Montcalm had destroyed the year before, he left all but 800 chosen men, who moved in row boats around the eastern shore of Lake Ontario, landed near Fort Frontenac, surrounded it, and received the surrender of 110 men. Sailors in boats in the harbor escaped, but they left nine sailing vessels armed with guns.

The Indians, wishing to kill the prisoners, suggested to Bradstreet: "Turn your back and shut your eyes like the French." But Bradstreet would have none of it. He provided an escort to take the prisoners back to Albany. He placated the Indians by giving them their choice of all the stores they could carry. He found great quantities of Indian gifts and trade goods as well as ammunition intended for shipment to Fort Duquesne. What he could not carry off, he destroyed, including seven of the ships, which he burned to the water's edge. The other two vessels he loaded with loot and sailed back to his main command.

To replace stores needed at Fort Duquesne, the governor of Louisiana directed the loading of a fleet of bateaux at New Orleans. In the beginning Canada had supplied Fort Duquesne, for while the French province of Louisiana covered most of the Mississippi Valley, the Upper Ohio was in Canada's realm. Canada, however, was pressed with threats from New York. More and more did Governor Vaudreuil withdraw the Canadian militia from Fort Duquesne for the St. Lawrence front. Consequently, when the war office in Paris learned that Forbes was leading an expedition westward from Pennsylvania, it commanded the governor of Louisiana to send replacements.

In consequence militia companies were dispatched from New Orleans, Kaskaskia, and Vincennes to the Forks of the Ohio. Louisiana, therefore, had a personal interest in sending supplies. A bateau on the Mississippi or the Ohio could be driven part of the time by sail. More often it was propelled by oars. At times when the swollen tide was too powerful for the oarsmen to make headway, the men of the crew tied one end of a *cordelle* to the mast and with the other leaped ashore to tow the craft by man power.

A horse drawing a canal boat had it easy compared with the cordelle men. The horse walked a towpath. The French *voyageurs* had no sign of a towpath on the river brink. They struggled over roots and fallen trees, around rocks and jutting bluffs, through vines and thorns, in water and mire. Fourteen and more hours a day their sweat fell like rain, while mosquitoes and buffalo gnats whined in their ears and sucked blood from their naked chests, and men boasted they had more endurance than an alligator. Mile after heartbreaking mile they heaved the *cordelle* as the helmsman, steering with the longoar lightened labor by leading them in nonsensical roundelays.

Captain Francois Marchaud de Ligneris, who had led a command at Braddock's defeat, and for three years had served under Dumas at Fort Duquesne, was now commandant. He was torn with anxiety, for his militia had enlisted only for the summer. Now it was harvest time and the men were surly, but he dared not send them home, for his scouts brought word that Bouquet, instead of going into winter quarters as any sensible general would, was relentlessly advancing.

To forget his despair, Ligneris, on many a night, after darkness had veiled the forest and the catamounts complained, drank himself drunk. But when a bateau or pirogue drew up from New Orleans to Duquesne's mud levee, he drank himself drunk to express his joy. He was able, however, to clear his head the next morning with another drink. Montcalm, hearing of how things fared at Duquesne, wrote a friend in France: "The Indians don't like Ligneris, who is drunk every day."

His scouts informed Ligneris that Bouquet, through August and early September, had hewn and graded a road from Rays-town to Loyalhanna, a distance of about 55 miles, although it is but 47 miles by U. S. Highway 30 today. They found the pass of the Alleghenies steeper than the same pass on Brad-dock's Road. Laurel Hill was still steeper. The scouts also brought an amusing tale. A large portion of Bouquet's troops were dressed as women. Why they suffered this humiliation puzzled the scouts. They could not understand that the High-landers took pride in their kilts, each of the same pattern as their plaids and all of the design of the clan to which each Scot belonged.

At Loyalhanna, so the scouts reported, Bouquet was build-ing a fort even greater than the one at Raystown. The maga-zines were greater. The barracks, storehouses, and hospitals were greater. Perhaps they were going to dig in for the winter.

XXV. *A Great Commando Raid*

WASHINGTON felt he was wasting his time. In mid-September an almost unbearable blow fell. Men of his regiment were led into battle and he was left at Cumberland instead of commanding them.

Among the Highlanders at Loyalhanna was Major James Grant, the favorite confidant of General Forbes. He was not interested in building forts. Like Washington he wanted to get on with the war. And so he talked Bouquet into letting him lead a commando raid on Fort Duquesne, which was 41 miles in a bee line and 56 miles away by the Raystown Path. Bouquet assigned to him 37 officers and 815 men, including in the party 300 Virginians under Major Lewis. Grant was directed by Bouquet not to make a direct assault on the fort itself, but to gather information and take prisoners.

Lewis, the only field officer there who had ever been to the area of Fort Duquesne, urged that the command was too small for a pitched battle and too large for gathering information. Give him a dozen Virginians and he promised to be back with information and prisoners. When Grant insisted he wanted to strike a blow that would elate the army and dishearten the enemy, and Bouquet supported him, Lewis said: "I want to make it a matter of record that I am opposed to the plan."

Each man carried a blanket, a white shirt, his weapons, ammunition, and rations. Supplementary ammunition and rations were packed on bat horses. Following the Raystown Path, the commandos arrived in what is now Pittsburgh the night of September 13 and rested a few hours.

At 2 o'clock in the morning, Grant roused the men. They heaped their blankets and other baggage, except the white shirts, on the ground and left the horses there. Grant detailed Captain Thomas Bullett and 50 Virginia veterans of three years of woods ranging as the horse and baggage guard.

With the rest Grant marched on about two miles more to a point that since has been called Grant's Hill. Here today passes Grant's Street, lined with office buildings and banks where big deals are transacted. Grant ordered all the men to don white shirts so they could identify their friends in the fighting he expected would ensue.

Following orders, Major Lewis led 250 Virginians down the hill, which was precipitous in places. It is less steep today for in 200 years the bluff's face has been scoured down as men have graded streets and leveled lots. It lacked three days of the full harvest moon and so the moon was setting as Lewis started on his mission. The men stumbled down in the darkness. In less than a mile they had reached the Monongahela bottom, where it was darker still, for a clammy fog shrouded the lowland. It was so dense men could not see each other more than a few feet away.

They made considerable noise as they floundered through a cornfield and came to a storehouse built to receive the harvest, but no sentry challenged them. Parties of men became separated from the main command and straggled back up the hill, much to the disgust of Grant. At length Lewis, who had no heart for the adventure, gave the order for a retrograde march back up Grant's Hill.

When he reported the scheme could not be carried out Grant contemptuously rasped that Lewis should lead all of his Virginians back to join Bullett and share the inglorious role of guarding the blankets and horses.

He did, however, offer Lewis an opportunity to redeem himself. Grant had a new scheme. He sent a small detachment down the hill to find the storehouse in the dark and set it afire. When the French sallied out to put out the fire, they would find the commandos, who would retreat up the hill to where Grant lay in wait behind trees. They were to race past the trees, drawing the French after them. As they sped past, the 400 men in ambush would open fire and kill at least 400 of the enemy.

Then if the French came in greater force than Grant could contain, he would retreat to where Lewis was in ambush and Lewis could redeem himself. It was simple enough if the enemy would only make the moves that Grant expected him to make.

The small detachment of commandos found the storehouse, struck a spark from a flint, and forthwith a fire crackled. As the commandos watched, a group of militiamen sortied from the fort and beat out the flames without suspecting that an enemy had set the fire. They did not even peer out into the fog to look for an enemy. As soon as they had the fire out, the militiamen trotted back to resume their snoring. The commandos, possibly relieved that they had not been discovered, climbed back to Grant to report what had happened.

Again Grant was out of sorts, but the lack of alertness on the part of the garrison put a fatuous notion into the major's head. Apparently he decided to assault the fort itself. He ordered a three-pronged advance. A company of 100 Pennsylvanians was commanded to take the right, a company of Scotch Highlanders the center, and another company of Highlanders the left.

On the hill Grant retained 250 Highlanders, Royal Americans, and Maryland militia and his Highland band of pipers and drummers. After giving time for the three companies to be near the fort, he directed the band to sound the reveille. At the word the bagpipes skirled and the drummers beat, and the garrison was at last thoroughly aware that an enemy was about. Ligneris leaped from bed, snorted down a drink, and improvised a battle plan. French regulars were sent to man the redoubts. Indians and militia scurried through the side gates, each group swarming about its captain or chief with no more military regularity than enraged hornets, but each hornet knowing that his job was to find a target.

Half dressed they ran, part following the banks of the Allegheny and part the Monongahela and still other parts, finding intervals between the attacking companies, filtered between. They encircled each company and even ascended Grant's Hill to encircle the force there. From the concealment of trees, each militiaman and Indian sighted his mark and fired at it. A captain of the Highlanders was killed and another captured.

Dawn broke and broadened into day as the men fought. By heroic endeavor each of the three companies, after suffering severe losses, fought its way back and reunited with Grant. For three quarters of an hour they fought on the hill. Lewis, hearing the firing, was undecided what to do. He had been directed to lay an ambuscade, but Grant did not retreat to him. Instead, he was trying to hold his army together so that it could more effectively fight its way out of the encircling militia and Indians.

Guessing what was detaining Grant, the Virginia non-commissioned officers and men begged Lewis to lead them to the rescue. Reluctantly, he did so, leaving Bullett at the baggage. Before Lewis could reunite with Grant, the outmaneuvered Highlanders broke and fled, joined by all the others. "I trust I shall never again see such panic among troops," lamented Grant.

Lewis, instead of following the more circuitous Raystown Path, marched in a straight line toward the sound of firing and in that way missed Grant's retreating troops. The French and Indians had a momentary shock when they encountered Lewis, for they had supposed that all of the troops were on the hill. They quickly recovered and surrounded the Virginians, who fought back as long as they could and then also retreated. The relentless enemy drove a part of the Virginians, Highlanders, and others into the Allegheny River.

"My heart is broken," exclaimed Grant. "I will not outlive this day." He did, however, outlive it. Both he and Lewis were captured and sent to Montreal.

The bulk of the flying commandos made for Bullett's position and arrived there. As they ran through Bullett's line, the Virginians remained in cover, but as the fugitive troops passed, Bullett's men began firing into the faces of the pursuers. At this unexpected action, the Indians, who made up most of the force confronting Bullett, took cover. To draw them out, Bullett directed his 50 men to rise and advance into the open with guns reversed in token of surrender.

The Indians, wholly deceived, came out from cover eager to grasp the guns and take the clothing of their captives. Thereupon Bullett ordered his men to fire, following the volley with a bayonet charge. At sight of the bristling bayonet points, the Indians fell back in confusion. The irresolution of the Indians lasted but a few moments, but it gave time for Bullett's men to reload and regain cover.

Other officers rallied their companies around Bullett and began an orderly withdrawal. A French officer called to Bullett, telling him he had no chance for escape and offering surrender. To this Bullett replied with a musket shot. Two thirds of his small force of 50 he left dead on the field. The Highlanders, who had previously looked down their noses at the Virginians in their hunting shirts, now looked to them for deliverance and later rated them as brothers.

The Indians, having won a substantial victory, gave over

the battle to scalp and strip the dead. The militia, without Indian help, hesitated to push on alone. The fact that Lewis and later Bullett had materialized from the forest indicated that perhaps still more commandos were veiled in ambush. They decided they had glory enough, and, like hornets, after driving off the enemy, returned to the fort, making horrible sounds on the captured bagpipes.

One Indian, having collected more property than he could carry, impaled the head of a scalped Highlander on the stub of a sapling to which he lashed the body. Then he draped the kilts about the legs to indicate that the soldier was a woman. Other Indians guffawed at the ghoulish joke. They, too, similarly mounted dead Highlanders and draped the kilts about their legs, but they carried away the plaids, wearing them on their shoulders in imitation of the Highlanders.

For three days the main force of the surviving commandos retreated to Loyalhanna. For several days more other survivors, who had swum the Allegheny or had been separated on the field, wandered in. Of 852 officers and men, 540 came back; 37 were captured and 275 dead. Reporting to Forbes, Bouquet wrote: "All probably would have been cut to pieces but for Captain Bullett and his Virginians who kept up the fight against the whole French force."

Forbes, lamenting the loss of Grant, answered that Grant had lost his wits and brought destruction on himself by his thirst for fame.

XXVI. *Throttled By Rain*

BULLETT'S leadership claimed the general's admiration and brought the truth to him that a Highlander, despite his courage and superiority in military training, was no match for a frontiersman in the woods. Commenting on this, Washington wrote to Fauquier: "Our officers and men have acquired very great applause for their gallant behavior during the action. I had the honor to be publicly congratulated yesterday by the General on the occasion."

Still tortured by dysentery, Forbes moved by short stages from Philadelphia to Carlisle and from Carlisle to Raystown, where he arrived September 17, arranging in advance for Washington to ride the 31 miles from Cumberland for a conference. This was their first meeting. The two officers were polite but reserved, each remembering their dispute over the road. Washington recognized at once that Forbes was dangerously ill. He could not ride a horse, and the jolting of a wagon released the devils of excruciating pain. Byrd was ill in bed and, therefore, failed to attend the conference, much to the general's disappointment. In the end Forbes directed Washington to return to Cumberland and bring the Virginians to Raystown.

Bouquet came from Loyalhanna to consult with Forbes at Raystown. Whether or not the scouts from Duquesne knew of Bouquet's departure is uncertain. We do know that Ligneris sent a force of 1000 men to attack Loyalhanna while Bouquet was on the other side of two ranges of mountains. Both Armstrong and Washington attended the conference as did other field officers. Armstrong was in favor with Forbes, for he had championed the cutting of a new road by way of Raystown Path.

Forbes was not easy at forgiveness, especially when he felt that an inferior had shown insubordination. At the same time the general recognized his own inexperience in woods warfare. He could not help knowing that the woods had ruined Braddock, Abercromby, and Grant. Perhaps this hulking Virginia colonel might have a suggestion. Throughout the discussion Washington spent most of his time listening. He had learned when serving under Braddock that it was the place of a provincial officer to keep his mouth shut unless asked for an opinion. He kept his mouth shut this time until Forbes asked if he had any ideas.

Sure he had ideas. He knew he was sticking his neck out to question the *modus operandi* of a British officer, and so he confined his recommendations as to how he would fight in the woods, without reference to fighting in general.

First he would decentralize authority so that every sergeant and corporal would have responsibility. If the army were broken into fragments, each fragment should fight on. If an attack came on a flank, that flank would be the front without wheeling the entire army. He would adopt the French and Indian enveloping tactics, so successful in their attack on Braddock and on Grant. He explained: "The first division, so soon as the vanguard is attacked is to file off to the right and left, and take to trees, gaining the enemy's flanks, and surrounding them, . . . which being a practice different from anything they have ever experienced from us, I think may be accomplished."

Forbes listened attentively. He knew from reports that Abercromby had attacked only at the front. Braddock had attacked only at the front. British tactics required a frontal attack. Washington may have argued that his noncommissioned officers as well as Armstrong's veterans had all commanded small details and had acquitted themselves well. He believed they could exercise responsibility when needed and that the British subalterns and noncommissioned officers could command as well as the provincial minor officers.

Forbes directed the colonel to put the plan in writing. Without a moment's hesitation the idea flowed off of Washington's pen to paper. As readily as he had sketched land plats when a surveyor, he now sketched a battle plan. The plan made sense, and Forbes adopted it.

The conference drew to a close and Bouquet started back toward Loyalhanna to prepare for the coming of the rest of the army, which was to advance on Duquesne from Loyalhanna. While Bouquet was still east of Laurel Hill, the thousand-man force sent by Ligneris, consisting of regulars, militiamen, and Indians, had arrived at Loyalhanna and launched an attack. Colonel James Burd of Pennsylvania, left by Bouquet in command, lost 62 in killed as he retired into the breastworks around the fort. The troops sent by Ligneris boldly attacked them there, pinning them down, while a flanking party shot and killed the beef herd, thereby destroying the fort's fresh beef supply. Indians also ran off a large part of the horse herd.

The French, having accomplished their objective, deliberately withdrew. They took time to bury their dead and carried off their wounded. Forbes complained because Burd failed to launch a counterattack as the enemy began to withdraw. Burd, however, knew when he was well off.

The plan for the removal of the army from Raystown to Loyalhanna called for an advance in units, each unit serving as a convoy for a wagon train. Washington was first to advance with two companies, marching out October 15.

The glory of autumn was upon the hills. All of the trees,

from oaks to chestnuts, from chestnuts to sassafras, were adorned in their royal robes. They put on deep red, light pink, gold, yellow, ocher, bronze, maroon, every gradation from deepest dye to the most delicate tint and shade. Amid the brightly colored trees stood the pines, cedars, firs, and hemlocks, like sentinels in green. Green, too, were the mountain holly, the thick leaved rhododendron, and the glossy laurel. In this art gallery hung by nature, the Virginia companies crossed the Alleghenies. To the west was Laurel Hill, with mists hanging over its summits portending a change in weather.

Next day the sorry clouds sobbed out rain in torrents. The spongy forest mast drank until it could contain no more and the overflow cascaded down the slopes. Where trees had been cut away for the road, the rain beat on the soft unprotected land, gouging ruts which eroded into gullies in a matter of hours.

Dry ravines bellowed like rivers and creeks roiled like tides of the sea. It was a most incessant rain, day following day. Rarely the clouds lightened just long enough for the sun to peep through, but it was only a mocking respite. The sun was soon veiled, and it rained the harder, drumming on the leaves, softening and loosening their petioles, thus hastening the falling of leaves in constant showers.

Horses could make scant headway. Hoofs and wagon wheels churned the mud into a quagmire. Men put shoulders to the wheels with grunt and heave, but even with help the spent animals stood trembling from weariness or fell prostrate. Soldiers cut saplings for levers to pry the horses back to their feet once more and could barely manage it. They put the sapling levers to the wheels while wagoners cracked their lashes, and the wheels sank to the linchpins.

Washington set his entire command, except those assigned to patrol duty, to making fascines. Small branches they had in plenty, which they bound into bundles with vines or withes of willow. These fascines they flung into mudholes, to afford a footing for the hoofs and a treadway for the tires.

The temperature dropped. The rain changed to a wet snow that plastered the laurel, melted on the shoulders of the men, and steamed from the backs of shivering horses. The horses needed food to provide the calories to withstand the cold. Although a large share of each load was food for the animals there was still insufficient corn and oats.

Now and then they came to a glade in the otherwise interminable forest. The horses chewed hungrily at the grass, but it was dead grass, dried with the coming of autumn. Unlike the farmer's hay, to which they were used, it was only roughage. Also unlike the hay, which the farmer mows when the meadows are abloom, and cures it in the windrow to retain as much as possible of the nutriment, this grass had, before it dried, sent its chlorophyll, vitamins, and succulence to the roots with the sap.

The men suffered with the horses. Washington and Byrd, not aware that Forbes had no plan for a summer campaign, had put their men in hunting shirts for hot weather. On these cold days they could keep warm by their unceasing exercise, but at night they huddled in their tents, lying close together so that no body heat would be lost. The cooks butchered cattle and the men gobbled fresh beef, salt pork, bread, meal, and beans. Never had Forbes known so few to eat so much. He complained of the gluttony of the Virginians, but remained a good provider as long as the roads held up.

At Laurel Hill came a new shock. The road was strangled in a pass that wound around a hill crowded between the bluff and the precipice of a ravine. Gaboons, built of riven staves like the walls of a bottomless barrel, into which were piled rocks and wood blocks, had been used by Bouquet's engineers to shore up the edges of the road. The never ending rain undermined the banks of the ravine and the gaboons slipped into the abyss.

Washington had to engineer a new road between the misty summits of Laurel Hill. This new road in the end proved to be shorter by four miles than the one laid out by way of the old Raystown Path. After nine days of most toilsome travel the men were cheered by the sight of smoke coming from the chimneys at Loyalhanna on the west foot of Laurel Hill.

In time the rest of the Virginians and the troops under Armstrong came through Washington's pass to Loyalhanna. Forbes came too, riding all of the way in a litter swung between two horses hitched tandem. He was terribly discouraged. True, the leaves were falling from the deciduous trees as the Pennsylvania traders had said, but the laurel and rhododendron thickets were as opaque with green as July. There were still many places where an enemy could attack from concealment. And the traders had never mentioned rain. To Pitt the general wrote a letter telling of his predicament. He feared he would be tied up in the mountains, from which he could not extricate his army.

Washington also took time to write an I-told-you-so letter to Fauquier. If Forbes had only listened and taken the Braddock Road, Fort Duquesne would long since have fallen, Washington wrote.

So bad was the Forbes Road that wagons sometimes could not make it through. On the other hand the French were getting supplies from New Orleans. Scouts reported to Forbes that 50 bateaux had unloaded untold tons of provisions at the Forks of the Ohio in late October.

Another thing worried Forbes. What if he did take Fort Duquesne? All the troops except the Highlanders, the 300 Royal Americans, and Washington's First Virginians were due to be discharged December 1. How could he garrison Fort Duquesne and keep the road policed with so few men? He wrote to the governors of Virginia and Pennsylvania imploring them to extend the enlistment date. Of course that was a proposal to break faith with men who had volunteered, but he must have men.

The governors had no authority to extend the enlistment, and the legislatures were reluctant. Indeed the Virginia Burgesses, disgusted that Forbes had not taken Braddock's Road, had passed a law in early fall requiring that the First Regiment be returned to Virginia on December 1. Fauquier, acting on the general's request, called the Burgesses into session in November. He was able to persuade them that nobody wanted the taking of Duquesne more than the Virginians. In mid-November the Burgesses passed the desired law to support the campaign, but the word did not reach Forbes until after November had gone, and he fumed his wrath.

As they lingered at Loyalhanna, waiting for the wagons to bring supplies and with the ragged provincials on short rations until the wagons did come, Washington gave up hope of taking Duquesne. Instead of going home to be married, he saw either the abandonment of Loyalhanna or himself sitting there inactive through the winter.

Forbes, however, had another trick. All through the summer he had pinned his hope on it. For three reasons he had deliberately slowed the advance on Duquesne. First, he was ill and hoped all the time he would recover. But he had not recovered and now was exposing his life to the elements as he swung helplessly in a litter. Second, he had thought the falling leaves would help. They had to some extent, but not enough. He had still a third hope to which he had clung all through his months at Philadelphia, at Carlisle, at Raystown and now at Loyalhanna. Would his third trick work?

XXVII. A Pacifist Enlists

EVER since his arrival in Philadelphia the previous April Forbes had given much consideration to a plan for winning the neutrality of the Ohio Indians. The thought originated the year before with Teedyuskung, a Delaware living in the Wyoming Valley, who styled himself the king of the Delawares, although his kingship was not recognized on the Ohio.

For a half century he had enjoyed the blessings of peace. Now 52 years old, he had for two years watched the Delaware, Mingo, and Shawnee scalping parties raid Pennsylvania and could not see that the raids benefited anybody. It was true, he argued, that his people had been wronged, but he believed he could gain more by negotiation than by the scalping knife.

He approached the Friends in Philadelphia, who introduced him to Governor Denny. The news that Pennsylvania was discussing peace with the Ohio Indians alarmed the Virginians. For several years they had been cultivating the friendship of the Catawabas and Cherokees and at last had won their alliance, not because they loved the English so much, but because they hated the Shawnees more.

The southern Indians had been at war with the Shawnees since long before the birth of the grandmother of the oldest living southern Indian. Now that the Delawares, Wyandottes, Miamis, and Mingoes were allied with the Shawnees, the southern Indians hated them all. To make peace with them would be quite likely to alienate the southern tribes from the English side, so the Virginians held.

In March, 1758, while Washington was convalescing at

Mount Vernon, Captain Thomas Bullett, commanding at Winchester, convened a council of officers at Fort Loudon where they prepared a memorial opposing the Teedyuskung plan. This they presented to the Virginia and Pennsylvania governments.

Forbes, however, coming to Philadelphia shortly after that, listened to the Friends, who proposed that no effort be made to win an alliance with the Ohio Indians, but that they instead should be asked to become neutrals. Forbes was interested in the somber-clad Friends, who kept on their hats when talking to him just to show that they recognized no superior but God. They did not even remove their hats in the presence of a king's personal representative, Governor Denny.

What Forbes did not know is that the Indians were democratic in their government. No king or chief told an Indian what to do unless the majority acquiesced. Questions of peace or war were decided in council. Even if the majority decided for peace, the minority might keep on fighting. He hoped there was a chance to retain the Catawabas and Cherokees as allies even if he neutralized the Ohio tribes. Even if he did not hold the southern Indians, he thought it worth the risk if he could wean away the allies of the French.

He therefore importuned Governor Denny to do all in his power to consummate a peace. Denny, knowing more about Indians than Forbes, was dilatory, while Forbes fretted. At long last, responding to the urgings of Forbes, the governor asked Christian Frederich Post, a Moravian missionary to the Delawares, to undertake a peace mission.

Post, a pacifist, had come to America from Germany 16 years before to escape conscription into the German army. During his 16 years he had lived with the Delawares of the Wyoming Valley. He learned their language, treated them as brothers, and married Rachael, an Indian woman. When she died in 1745, he mourned for two years. Then he married Agnes, another Christian Delaware.

The Friends advised Denny that no other white man held the affection of Delawares, Shawnees, and Mingoes so completely as Post. The Moravian, however, demurred. He told Denny that the acceptance of a commission from the governor "would be out of the way of a minister of the Gospel." "Yet he yielded thereto," so Denny related, "on its being argued that the bringing about of a Peace with the Indians would open the way for Servants of God to look for a future harvest."

With funds provided by the governor, Post employed three Delawares, all good hunters. They rode horseback, carrying limited supplies in their saddlebags, for they expected to subsist on the way to the Indian nations by hunting, and after arrival by enjoying the hospitality of the red men. Post had cause later to regret his selection of one of the Delawares, Shamokin Daniel, whom he was to describe thus: "Daniel is a very false fellow, speaks for the English when with the English and for the French when with the French."*

The embassy traveled without important incident until it arrived at the ford of the Allegheny River opposite Venango, where the French had built a fort and had a small garrison. Before crossing, Post entered in his journal: "I prayed the Lord to Blind them as he did the enemies of Lot and Elisha that I might pass unknown." After his prayer, he and his Delawares crossed the river. As they came up the west bank, they were accosted by two French soldiers, who talked with the Delawares, but apparently did not notice the white man, for his journal says: "The Lord heard my prayer and I passed unknown."

---

* Quotations from Post, Forbes, and others in this chapter are from *Pennsylvania Archives*, Vol. III, Philadelphia, 1853, and from Post's original letters as printed in the appendix from Daniel W. Kaufman, *Early History of Western Pennsylvania*, Pittsburgh, 1846.

From Venango the envoys followed the trace to Kuskuskung, a village of log houses on Beaver River west of the capital village of Logstown. As they approached the village they fell in with several Shawnee and Delaware warriors who formerly had lived in eastern Pennsylvania and recognized Post. They led the party to the house of King Beaver, the leading Delaware warrior there, and introduced Post as a man of God. To King Beaver Post directed a speech, the purport of which was: "We do not want to hurt you, because we love you. We, therefore, ask that you withdraw from Fort Duquesne so that when the English army comes you will not be killed."

King Beaver entertained the embassy at his own house, but he could not determine what to answer. And so he took Post and his companions to Logstown to confer with Chief Shingiss there. Here Post encountered open hostility on the part of young warriors. "I could see a denial of my Life in their Countenances," he wrote.

Shingiss protected Post, but he realized that he could not resolve the question of peace and war. That had to be done in a council of warriors. He therefore prevailed on Post to do a very daring thing. He offered to take him to the Indian camp beside Fort Duquesne itself. Post knew the danger. In his journal he wrote: "Whenever I looked towards that place I felt a dismal impression, the very place seemed shocking and dark."

Nevertheless, having agreed to go to the Ohio, he would not brush danger aside. To Fort Duquesne he went, accompanied by Shingiss and Beaver. Captain Ligneris could not go into the Indian camp and seize Post, for the missionary was a guest of two important chiefs who would have been offended had the French taken summary action. A French soldier, therefore, was sent to beguile Shamokin Daniel into visiting the commander in the fort. There Ligneris presented him with a gold-laced coat, a hat, a blanket, a shirt, ribbons, a new gun, and powder and lead. Daniel strutted back, announcing that the English had never given him anything, but the French had proved by their gifts that they were friends. He conspired with other Indians to help him kidnap Post from the camp and deliver him to Ligneris.

Before he could accomplish this, the head warriors assembled for a council, which Post addressed in the Delaware tongue, telling the Indians how the English loved the Indians and did not ask them to go to war on their side, because they did not want them to be killed. All the English asked was that the Indians withdraw from Fort Duquesne while General Forbes advanced with his great army. By such a withdrawal, the Indians would not be killed. To this Daniel shouted: "Why don't you and the French fight on the sea? You come here only to cheat the Indians and take their land."

The speech swayed Shingiss, who added: "We have good reason to believe you intend to drive us away and settle the country; or else why do you come to fight in the land that God has given us?"

Unable to gain anything, the council broke up, and Post returned to Kuskuskung. He remained there three weeks without making progress. In his journal he commented: "It's a Troublesome Cross & Heavy Yoke to Draw his people. They pinch & Squeeze a body's heart to the Utmost."

While Post was staying at Kuskuskung, Grant was defeated in his raid against Fort Duquesne. This turned the warriors against the peace proposal. They decided that Forbes must not be much of a general. Post, consequently, left Kuskuskung three days after Grant's defeat. As he departed King Beaver invited him to come again, advising him to leave Daniel at home, and, instead, to bring some English officers as evidence of their love for the Indians.

Veering wide of Fort Duquesne, Post reached the Pennsylvania frontier safely. After he had arrived at the frontier settlements and had crossed to the east bank of the Susquehanna River, he encountered 20 Delaware and Mingo warriors, carrying a scalp and leading five civilian prisoners they had taken in a raid on the white settlements in eastern Pennsylvania.

He camped with them all night and tried to persuade them to free the prisoners, but without success. The next morning he parted from the warriors, who went west with their prisoners, while Post reported the failure of his expedition to Governor Denny.

Denny, prodded by Forbes, called a council at Easton, to which came Delaware, Shawnee, and Mingo warriors from eastern Pennsylvania and also a large party of Iroquois from New York under the tutelage of Sir William Johnson, who acted under pressure of Forbes.

Teedyuskung told the council that the greatest barrier to peace was the action of the Iroquois, who had sold land in the Wyoming Valley to agents from Connecticut. The Delawares no longer were women, he asserted. The Iroquois had no longer any right to sell land belonging to the real people.

The Iroquois, at the insistence of Johnson, agreed to wash away the sale. Teedyuskung was placated and led the Indians present in writing a peace. This accomplished, Denny sent Post a second time to go behind the French lines to acquaint the Indians of the Ohio with what had been accomplished at Easton and to ask that they ratify the Easton peace.

On his second mission Post took several Delaware friends, leaving Daniel at home. He also had Denny send two Pennsylvania officers. The party arrived at Loyalhanna November 7 and spent two nights there, the center of a curious group.

An officer asked Post: "How could you rule and bring these people to reason without gun or sword?"

To this the Moravian answered: "It is done by no other power than faith."

Forbes drew up a letter for Post to read to the Indians. Its language is so much like Post's that it is probable that the peacemaker had a hand in preparing it. The nub of the letter reads: "Let the French fight their own battles, as they were the first cause of the War and the occasion of the long differences which hath existed between you and your brothers the English, but I entreat you to restrain your young men from crossing the Ohio, as it will be impossible for me to distinguish them from our enemies; which I expect you will comply with without delay, lest I should be the innocent cause of our brethren's death. I write to you as a warrior should with candor and love."

At his meeting with Forbes, Post gave the general the information that the French had 1400 regular soldiers and militiamen at Fort Duquesne besides 1600 Indians, either at the fort or at villages nearby, who could be summoned quickly. Forbes was very much discouraged at the news. He did not see how he could attack 3000 people.

What was troubling him more was the fact that rains had delayed the arrival of wagons. The men were on short rations. He therefore concluded that his best hope was to win the neutrality of the Ohio Indians. He assigned an escort of 15 men, commanded by Lieutenant Hay, to take Post's embassy as far as the Allegheny River. This was to protect Post from French and Indian patrols lying in wait around Loyalhanna. Post accepted the escort with reluctance and eventually had reason to believe that he would have fared as well without the soldiers.

Fortunately Post's party left the Raystown Path shortly after leaving Loyalhanna, for at the same time that Post was leaving Loyalhanna, an expedition was leaving Fort Duquesne, which moved eastward along the Raystown Path. This expedition was sent out by Ligneris to do what damage it could at Loyalhanna and discourage the English from a further advance.

It was made up of militiamen and Indians. According to Post 160 warriors from Kuskuskung were in the expedition, which probably included King Beaver. When Hay reached the Allegheny River north of Fort Duquesne, he turned back while Post and his party followed the Kuskuskung trace. Arriving at Kuskuskung, Post found only two old men besides women and children. There was nothing he could do but wait for the warriors to return.

The raid on Loyalhanna was repulsed with considerable loss. The Indians were on their way home in a vengeful mood when they ran into Hay and his escort returning from the Allegheny River. In a short battle, they killed five men, including Lieutenant Hay. They took five prisoners while five escaped by running. The prisoners were taken by warriors from Kuskuskung, who journeyed home, intending to kill the five by torture.

Imagine their astonishment when they found Post and two Pennsylvania officers in their village! Their attitude was so threatening that one of the officers trembled with fear. Post calmed him with the words: "As God hath stopped the mouths of lions, that they could not devour Daniel, so he will preserve us from their fury."

The older Indians recognized Post as an ambassador and offered him and his companions protection. Post could not stand silent and watch his former guards be tortured. He pleaded: "Consider, my brethren, if you should give us a guide to bring you safe on your way home, and our parties should fall into you, how would you like it?"

A French soldier present suggested that they knock Post in the head. To this a warrior answered: "If you wish to go to war, go to the English army and knock them in the head, and not these three men, who come with a message to us."

While sparing the envoys the Indians made ready to torture Sergeant Henry Osten, one of the five prisoners. They first had him run the gauntlet, in which he sped past more than 200 men and women to reach the house where Post was quartered. "It is a grievous and melancholy sight," wrote Post, "to see our fellow mortals so abused."

The warriors came into the house to drag the beaten and bleeding Osten to a torture fire. Here the two Pennsylvania officers intervened. With such goods as they had in their saddlebags, they bought the freedom of all of the prisoners.

Post now counseled with the Indians. Day after day they met with no result. He read the letter from Forbes, but a French officer asserted that Forbes was making double talk. Forbes had written a far different letter that had been taken from the body of Lieutenant Hay. In this letter, so the officer asserted, Forbes had said that as soon as he had driven out the French, he would kill the Indians and take their land.

Post charged the officer with falsehood and demanded to see the letter. The officer explained that the letter was at the fort and, therefore, could not be read. As they argued the Indians wavered between their desire for peace and their distrust of the English.

Shingiss tried to exact a pledge from Post that the English army would withdraw across the mountains after it had defeated the French. But Post knew the English would not withdraw. The most he could pledge was that he would discuss the matter with Forbes after the peace was signed. With that the conference was stymied. It required all of Post's patience to maintain a semblance of good humor. November was drawing to a close. Post prayed, but his prayers seemed to go unanswered.

XXVIII. *Ligneris Undoes Himself*

WHILE Post was trying with little success to incline the council at Kuskuskung to peace, other forces were in motion to help him. It will be remembered that Post shocked Forbes when he told him that Ligneris could muster 3000 French and Indians for the defense of Fort Duquesne.

This information, coupled with the difficulty in rationing his army and the additional fact that most of the provincials would go home December 1, sank Forbes in gloom. He summoned a council of field officers, who agreed that they would be lucky to hold Loyalhanna through the winter without trying to reach Fort Duquesne.

Washington was downcast by the decision, and yet he had predicted it as early as September. It meant that he would have to postpone marriage another year, for honor would not let him resign his command until Duquesne had fallen.

Had Lingeris only known of the decision of the council, he could have spared himself the effort of calling on the Indians to help him with a raid against Loyalhanna, the object being to dishearten the English and keep them where they were or impel them to withdraw. Only a few hundred Indians came. The Wyandottes and Miamis were widely scattered for their fall hunt. The Delawares, Shawnees, and Mingoes also were hunting, but they sent a few hundred warriors.

These were sufficient, so Ligneris hoped, to destroy the beef herd, kill the horses, and perhaps carry off as many scalps as his men had done in the October raid before it was repulsed by Colonel Burd. His commando group, numbering 500 white and red men, left Duquesne at about the same time as Forbes was holding his council.

Among the raiders, Ligneris sent a Pennsylvania prisoner named Johnson, an agreeable chap, who, since his imprisonment, had convinced the French that he was a collaborator. He doubtless was sent along because he could speak English without a French accent. Perhaps he could decoy some of the English soldiers into an ambuscade. At least he could hear the commands of the officers and interpret them.

The probability is that the French intended to scout Loyalhanna thoroughly by moonlight, since it was the light of the moon, and be ready to attack at dawn, for the Indians did not fight at night except under compulsion. Consequently it was late afternoon when they arrived.

Whatever their plan, the alert patrols about the camp discovered them and alarmed headquarters. Forbes, thinking it was only a small party, ordered Lieutenant Colonel George Mercer, commanding the Second Virginia Regiment in the absence of Colonel Byrd, to take 500 men, almost exactly as many as the French and Indians had, and drive the prowlers away.

Mercer attacked with such vigor and skill that he drove the resisting enemy back about three miles when they broke and fled. At the fort Washington listened with mounting anxiety as the sound of firing receded in the distance. Fearing that Mercer might be running into a trap, he begged Forbes for permission to follow as a supporting unit. Permission granted, Washington sallied out with 500 men of his own regiment. By the time he had covered the three miles, the dusk of evening was dimming the forest. Mercer's men, seeing a force coming on the double-quick, mistook them in the encircling dark for a detail of the enemy that had gotten between them and the fort.

The Second Virginians opened fire and the First Virginians replied. Washington rushed between the two lines, crying out not to shoot. Forty years later, he recalled: "I never was in more imminent danger, by being between the two fires, knocking up with a sword the presented pieces."

In a moment the firing ceased, but that day Virginia lost 14 killed and 26 wounded, nearly all in the brief fight between themselves. Official reports indicate that the French lost only one killed and three captives. We know the losses must have been more than that, because of the spirit of vengeance displayed by the Indians at Kuskuskung as witnessed by Post.

Washington and Mercer were mortified that their own men should accidentally shoot each other, but there came a consoling event. A patrol of Virginians had come upon four persons in the woods sitting by a fire. They included one Frenchman, two Indians, and Johnson, the Pennsylvanian prisoner. They had been detached from the main body to go on a scout. As the French and Indian forces fled before Mercer's attack, the four failed to be reunited with them. Apparently they had decided to bivouac for the night, when they were betrayed by the light of their fire.

As a patrol was about to surround them, the Frenchman attempted to escape and was killed. The two Indians and Johnson surrendered. Washington directed that the three captives be questioned separately regarding the strength of Fort Duquesne. Johnson was under suspicion, for why would he be with the enemy on a raid unless he was a collaborator?

Johnson told an apparently truthful story. He said that since Post had been at Fort Duquesne, most of the militiamen had gone home. Fort Duquesne, instead of having 1400 white men, had only about 500. The Indians, busy with hunting, were mostly gone. They would be hard to assemble quickly, for they were widely scattered.

The Indians, questioned separately, corroborated Johnson in every essential detail. Of course, Washington lost no time in reporting back to Forbes. He showed that now was the time to strike instead of waiting until spring. Forbes, with his usual caution, was not sure of Johnson's loyalty, but since the Indians bore him out, Forbes decided that it was a good gamble that Johnson was telling the truth.

The next morning, November 13, with only 17 days left until the bulk of the provincial troops should be discharged, Forbes gave the order for Washington and Armstrong with 1000 Virginians and 1000 Pennsylvanians to build a road to Fort Duquesne. Washington was made acting brigadier general.

Probably no road has ever been built through a forest in such a hurry. Axes were dull and had not been ground. In many instances the helves were split or broken. All told only 42 new axes were supplied. But these men knew how to make the most of the tools they had. They knew how to carve new helves from a piece of hickory. They had begun swinging an ax while they still had their milk teeth. They were the most skilled axmen in the world, and now that power saws are used to fell trees in the logging camps, the world probably never will see their like again.

As they advanced they set the earth atremble with the crashing of virgin oaks, walnuts, hickories, chestnuts, beeches, buckeyes, elms, maples, basswoods, sycamores, pines, cedars, hemlocks, and firs. While those most skilled at felling were bringing down the trees, others were firming the mud holes with fascines, shoring up the edges of the roadway with gaboons, and corduroying the crossings of sloughs and creeks with logs laid transverse to the roadway and weighted into place with stones or pinioned there with stakes. Other men chopped away thickets of laurel and rhododendron, which might serve as hiding places for skulking Indians.

While part of the men swung axes, others stood at arms, muskets primed and loaded, ready for action at the word. The workingmen, too, kept weapons at hand. On either side of the roadway and to the fore, videttes patrolled the woods. Washington and Armstrong were everywhere, by voice and demeanor encouraging the men to hurry, hurry, hurry.

The method of procedure was for Armstrong, with his thousand Pennsylvanians, to march a distance down Raystown Path. There he had his men build a redoubt under the direction of a British engineer. It was sometimes a set of two or three block houses or stockades. One of the three structures was roofed and equipped with a chimney and fireplace, where the general might rest in warmth as he moved forward by easy stages as the road was opened.

As soon as the redoubt was finished, Armstrong's men began building the road, working toward Washington's position. When the men met at the close of the first day, they had converted six miles of Raystown Path into the Forbes Road. A company of Highlanders took over the redoubt to serve as a wayside rallying place in the event of an attack.

The second day they cleared eight miles and bivouacked that night amid the snow-blanketed escarpments of Chestnut Ridge. They had no tents, for Forbes, knowing it was more important to provide food, could spare no wagon to haul tents. The men, therefore, threw up makeshift half-faced camps or slept in the open before fires.

Fortunately, the rains abated, making it less uncomfortable to sleep out. It helped the wagon trains too, and more food could be brought over Laurel Hill to the ravenous army.

Washington fed his men in three days the bullocks that Forbes intended for four. Some men groused that the commissary detail, in cutting up the meat, gave larger portions to others. To answer their complaints, Washington requisitioned from Forbes a steelyard for every commissary sergeant so that the meat could be weighed before the eyes of the men.

And still they grumbled, but they vied with each other in work. Fellers raced to see who could topple the greatest number of trees in a day, and at night would brag of their prowess. They worked as long as daylight served. Breakfast was eaten before day. They had their noon meal while leaning on their ax helves. Night comes early to the Ohio headstreams in mid-November, and supper was not eaten until it was dark.

After supper the men whetted the bits of their axes, to have them well edged against the next day's task. The column that advanced to build the next redoubt, marched out long before daylight to be on the site at the break of dawn.

Washington complained to the engineer about building the walls at a stockade or blockhouse straight up and down. That might do in Europe, but here an Indian could slip up to the wall in the night and, set it afire or, if there was light, shoot through the loopholes on the men inside. Who was Washington, a mere surveyor, to tell an engineer how to build? Both Washington and Armstrong had been building frontier forts for a long time. Washington had been at it since he ordered the building of Necessity four and a half years before. He argued that a redoubt should have a wedge shaped ravelin of logs and earth breast high or, better still, head high, thrust out as a salient from the walls. Then a soldier in the ravelin could see the outside walls of the redoubt and enfilade an enemy lurking there.

Whether his disagreement with the engineer was the cause, Washington changed places with Armstrong. He marched ahead and helped the engineer construct the redoubts. By traveling the Raystown Path, the road builders missed all the rivers. They left Loyalhanna Creek when they began the ascent of Chestnut Ridge, and the Loyalhanna veered to the north. The biggest water they crossed was Turtle Creek, going over it about 20 miles northeast of where its high bluffs defied Braddock and caused him to bypass three and a half years before.

After eleven days of road building, the brigade had advanced about 45 miles from Loyalhanna, building nearly as many miles of road in eleven days as Bouquet's brigade had built in six weeks. They were now twelve miles from Fort Duquesne. The nearer they came, the greater were their precautions. Washington and Armstrong saw to it that every man knew exactly the part he would take in case of a battle. Nobody was to be surprised.

At this point Forbes caught up with the road brigade and spent the night by the fireplace in the foremost redoubt. With the arrival of Forbes the spirits of the men rose. True, he was desperately ill and had to ride in a litter. True, he issued an order that any man who fired his musket without command should suffer 200 lashes on the bare back. True, he ordered that all the men who had brought their pet dogs must hang the dogs or send them back to Loyalhanna. These rigid rules were issued to prevent the betrayal of their position, but it was an unneeded precaution; the enemy knew all about the advance of the army.

Men spent the evening about the fires, grumbling at the orders. They shivered in their summer uniforms through the night, but they arose the next morning with joy in their hearts. At long last they were going to fight. The veterans of Braddock's disaster would be avenged. The recruits were going to play hero roles. They bragged about how they would shoot and kill.

The morning of November 24, Forbes ordered the advance to stop. Men were to remain at camp until the rest of the army arrived that afternoon. The men were to rest and be in perfect physical condition for the advance that was to start without a road the next day.

Forbes called his field officers to a conference in his blockhouse. The fire crackled on the hearth in the stone fireplace built only the day before. The mud, which served as plaster, was dried by the heat of the fire that had burned all night.

The general ordered that the army would march next day in three columns. Washington would lead the left column, composed of troops from Delaware, Maryland, the Carolinas, and Virginia. Bouquet would take the right, leading the Pennsylvanians and Royal Americans. Lieutenant Colonel Archibald Montgomery would command the Highlanders, who would form the middle column and handle the artillery.

There was no wagon train to protect. The wagons and dogs were all sent back to Loyalhanna. Each man was issued six days' rations, which he carried in his hunting shirt or jacket. There were no tents. This would be a fighting army with every man carrying his own ammunition.

Forbes had with him George Croghan, who commanded a small detail of Cherokee and Catawaba scouts. Croghan was directed by Forbes to have the scouts reconnoiter the enemy and report back that afternoon. The scouts departed.

Darkness fell and still no word came of the scouts. Were the French and Indians on the way to meet him? Were they planning to make a stand in front of the fort? What was going on? Had the scouts been cut off? After accounting for the sick and the men manning the forts and the wayside redoubts, Forbes had 4200 men, all burning with eagerness to fight, but what was the matter with the intelligence? Why didn't the scouts return?

XXIX. *Twelve Miles To Go*

CROGHAN'S Indian scouts, whose day-long absence was fretting Forbes, were soft-footing it through the forest without finding an enemy. Since they found none, they kept on searching until late in the afternoon, when some of them, if not all, stole to the hills overlooking Fort Duquesne and saw a performance so unexplainable that curiosity riveted their feet to where they stood.

They saw the French, busy as ants, stripping the thatch and shake roofs from the huts outside the stockade and carrying the material inside to strew it over the floors or against the walls of buildings and against the stockade itself. Since it had not rained for several days, the thatch was dry and inflammable. The roofing moved, the Frenchmen opened the river gates and loaded the bateaux at the levee. Then, as darkness settled, they boarded all the bateaux but one and pushed from shore.

The single bateau at the levee was held as passage for a few arsonists, who scurried about touching torches to the thatch and shakes taken from the roofs. As tongues of yellow licked their way up the walls, the arsonists ran to the waiting boat, leaped aboard, and pushed off as though pursued by demons. The bateau carrying militiamen from Louisiana floated down the Ohio. Those carrying the French regulars and the Canadians breasted the Allegheny with sweep of oars. All this was made visible by the brightening glare of the burning fort, which floodlighted the stage.

In a few minutes the reason for the haste of the last bateau became apparent. The men had laid a trail of powder to serve as a fuse to entice the flames into a magazine. From the instant the fire touched the open fuse, it was but a whiff of time until it raced to the magazine. The explosion deafened the ears of the watching scouts and was heard as a dull boom by the army twelve miles away. From a roaring, seething caldron of flame there swelled a frightening billow of red, orange, and amber, leaping higher than the trees atop the hills. Some of the awe-struck Indians had seen enough. They raced to tell Forbes.

Others descended to the clearing to approach the fire as near as the heat would permit. They saw that not a Frenchman was about. Then they, too, retired to tell the story to the general. Apparently they stopped to sleep on the way, for it was day before they arrived. They said that everything had burned except the huts outside the stockade.

The news alarmed Forbes. He had counted on occupying the fort as a shelter for his garrison during the winter. The huts must be saved by all means. He, therefore, called the vedettes, whom he had designed to screen his advance, and directed that they ride with all speed to prevent the fire from spreading to the huts. He warned the horsemen to be constantly alert. If the French and Indians appeared, the vedettes were to retreat instead of risking battle. True the scouts had seen the French depart, but who can tell in war whether an enemy is merely feigning flight? What was to hinder them from landing their boats and returning through the woods to wreak what destruction they could?

As the cavalry trotted off, Forbes directed the army to form and march according to the plan outlined the day before. Foot patrols were flung out to cover the flanks and the advance as well as to bring up the rear.

Cautiously the troops moved in regular order, until in the early afternoon they came to the scene of Grant's defeat. The sight of heads impaled on sapling pikes, and of kilts draped around the leg bones as the Indians had arranged them in September, threw the Highlanders into a frenzy. The implication that the Indians regarded the Highlanders as petticoat soldiers was instantly grasped. Drawing sabers and casting all discipline aside, the Scots ran forward, uttering threats of vengeance. They outran the patrols. Hardly could Montgomery and his officers restore the men to their regular formation.

As the army descended Grant's Hill, none needed to be told that the cavalry had arrived too late to save the huts. Only 30 blackened chimneys remained to show where shelter had stood. Some of the men, poking among the embers of the fort, recoiled in surprise. They had looked into a second powder magazine that had not been exploded. Fearing that it might go off in their faces and blow them to meet their Maker, some withdrew. The less cautious ones reasoned that since the magazine had not exploded while the fort was in flames, it would not explode from the heat of the cooling embers. They entered the magazine and found it had been well protected with earthen embankments and roof to prevent the English from exploding it by shell fire from the outside.

This same embankment and roof had saved it from the flames of the burning fort. A trail of powder had been laid as a fuse into the magazine, but apparently the sputtering sparks had snuffed out before entering the magazine itself. Sixteen barrels of dry powder they found there.

Never did an army, after four years of struggle, accept a victory with less enthusiasm. These men had come keyed for battle. They came with faith they could make the French and Indians pay in blood. Now, after all their hardship, they had captured only the frozen ground. Yet Forbes and his colonels knew that it was better to win without the loss of life. The Forks of the Ohio were at last English. The bloodless triumph impelled Bouquet to write a victory letter to be carried back to Philadelphia without delay. Concluding he added: "After God, the success of this expedition is entirely due the General, who, by bringing about the treaty with the Indians at Easton, struck the French a stunning blow, wisely delayed our advance to wait the effects of the treaty, secured all our posts and left nothing to chance, and resisted the urgent solicitation to take Braddock's road, which would have been our destruction. In all his measures he has shown the greatest prudence, firmness, and ability."

General Forbes was too ill and too cold to write that day. Before the sun set the colonial axmen felled suitable trees, cut them into logs, built a blockhouse, plastered a chimney with mud and laid a fire on the fireplace. The general, for one, was carried from his litter to the warmth of a hut, while the provincials shivered in their worn hunting shirts as they bedded down for the night on that boreal but historic November 25.

The next day Forbes ordered the start of three work projects. He put one crew to building a road from the ruined fort to the redoubt twelve miles away. He set a second to building a great stockade with ravelins. It would serve as a fort until Stanwix could come the next spring and build Fort Pitt. A third group began building huts inside the stockade to house a garrison.

Along in the morning, Forbes took out time from construction to assemble the men for a Thanksgiving ceremony conducted by the Reverend Charles Beatty, a Presbyterian chaplain of a Pennsylvania regiment. The ceremony was designed to impress on the soldiers and also on the Indians, who were watching from across the river, that the English had won a great victory.

As a feature of the program, Forbes ordered the raising of a British flag over the ruins of Fort Duquesne as a symbol of victory. Contemporary Virginia historians, who had firsthand access to the truth, state that to Washington was assigned the honor of raising the flag. Pennsylvania historians, with equal opportunity to know the truth, have it that Armstrong raised the flag. Since both Virginia and Pennsylvania claimed the Forks of the Ohio, there was a reason for this difference. If Forbes had assigned the raising of the flag to Washington, it would indicate that he felt Virginia had the better claim to the Forks. If Armstrong raised the standard, it would strengthen the Pennsylvania claim. In his letter to Pitt, Forbes merely indicated that the flag was floating over the ruins.

The flag raising over, the men resumed their work of construction. From time to time that day groups of Delawares, Shawnees, and Mingoes, who had fought on the side of the French, now came to shake hands with the English and to pledge fealty to the winner. They brought the news that Ligneris had gone to Venango, where the French had set up a sawmill and had built barracks of sawed lumber. Before departing, Ligneris told the Indians he would return with an army to dislodge the English. The Indians, however, had counted the English and cast their lot with the greatest number.

On the second day, Forbes detailed a party of Highlanders to bury their dead countrymen on Grant's Hill. A detail of provincials, commanded by a Pennsylvania captain, he dispatched to perform a like service for those who died at Braddock's defeat. Indians, who had fought on the side of the French in the Battle of the Monongahela, guided them to the scene. Accompanying the party was Major Halkett, who hoped to find the remains of his father and brother. An Indian warrior led Halkett to a tree he remembered well. He had seen a colonel fall and die there. A young ensign, whom the Indian took for the colonel's son, had run to the older man and bent over him. As he stooped, he, too, was killed and fell across his father's body, so the Indians said.

Workmen raked aside the leaves that had accumulated through four autumns and uncovered two skeletons, one lying across the other. Halkett examined the teeth of the one beneath, for his father had one false tooth. Sure enough, he found the tooth he sought. This was the skeleton of his father, Sir Peter Halkett, and the other must be that of the major's brother James. The major was so emotionally moved that he fainted, falling beside his father and brother.

After he revived, the men dug a grave into which they laid the bones of the father and son, draping them with a plaid of the Halkett clan before covering with earth. The rest of the bones they placed in a long trench, covered them, and read a belated service over them.

On November 27, two days after his arrival at the Forks, the general was able to write to Pitt. The victory had been won, he reported. A small settlement of huts, surrounded by a stockade, was under construction. This he named Pittsburgh and suggested to the Prime Minister that it might some day become a great city. He also announced to Pitt that he had changed the name of Raystown to Bedford and Loyalhanna to Ligonier to flatter two influential friends of Pitt.

Through all of this time Post was at Kuskuskung conferring with the Indians regarding peace. Late in the afternoon of November 25 a runner came to Kuskuskung to report that Ligneris had fled to Venango. Shingiss still insisted that the English must agree to withdraw to the east of the mountains. This Post would not promise, for he had no authority to offer a withdrawal. In the end Shingiss yielded and on November 28 signed the peace agreement, accepting Post's word that he would request Forbes to withdraw.

Post had the satisfaction, in the final conference, of obtaining the letter a French officer had asserted was written by Forbes and which stated that the English would destroy the Indians after defeating the French. The letter proved to be one written by Post himself. He had given it to Lieutenant Hays to carry to Forbes. Post now demanded that the letter be read aloud and translated by Isaac Still, a Christian Delaware who could read English and who was one of Post's party. The reading of the letter convinced the Indians that Forbes had no intention of destroying them.

The Forks in English hands, Forbes knew it was time to pay attention to his health. Recovery, he felt, could best be won in Philadelphia. Writing to Governor Denny, he said: "I kiss your Hands, and flatter myself that if I get to Philadelphia, and under your cares and good Companys, I shall yet run a good Chance of re-establishing a Health that I run the risque of ruining to give your Province all the Satisfaction of my weak Abilities."

Before he could leave, Forbes had to assign troops to garrison Pittsburgh through the winter. Because of the difficulty of hauling supplies over the mountains, he felt that he could not maintain more than 350 men. The remainder had to be moved out as rapidly as possible, as food for men and horses had been consumed faster than could be brought through. He also needed to assign men to the fort at Loyalhanna and the one at Raystown.

"We would soon make M. de Ligneris shift his quarters at Venango if we only had provisions," Bouquet lamented to a friend in Philadelphia, "but we are scarcely able to maintain ourselves a few days here."*

---

* Quotations from Bouquet's letter are from Parkman, *Montcalm and Wolfe*.

The Forbes letter is from Minutes of the Provincial Council of Pennsylvania, Vol. III, p. 233, Harrisburg, 1852.

Forbes realized that the provincials could best cope with contingencies that might arise in this strange place. Further, they were the best men with the ax and pike pole, who could be relied on to fell timber and roll it to the site of a proposed Fort Pitt, which Stanwix would build when spring came. The men to garrison Pittsburgh, Loyalhanna, and Raystown had to come from such provincial troops as could be persuaded to volunteer in addition to the Royal Americans and the First Virginians. Washington protested that the king's troops should guard the forts; besides his men were not clothed for winter. But Forbes had his mind made up, and Washington, knowing that he could not change that stubborn mind, wrote for winter clothing to Governor Fauquier. "I endeavored to show," he told the governor, "that the King's troops ought to garrison it; but he told me . . . he could not order it, and our men that are left there, are in such a miserable situation, having hardly rags to cover their nakedness, exposed to the inclemency of the weather in this rigorous season."

Washington had let it be known early in the campaign that he would resign his commission as soon as Fort Duquesne had fallen. He, therefore, was not available as commandant at Pittsburgh or the projected Fort Pitt. Forbes, therefore, named Colonel Hugh Mercer of Pennsylvania to command.

This done, he directed Washington to ride to Williamsburg with all speed where he could personally expedite the transport of winter clothing for his men at Pittsburgh. The troops not detailed to remain were ordered to march east with haste so as to conserve food and fodder. Arrangements completed, he took his departure, riding all the way to Philadelphia in his horse-borne litter. He received the "cares and companys" that Philadelphia could provide, but he had "risked" too much. Week by week he grew worse, and in March he died.

XXX. *Rainbows in Their Eyes*

BY TAKING Fort Duquesne the English had broken the heart of France and wrecked its central bastion. In less than a year letters from the north would bear tidings to Washington of how Wolfe ascended to the rear of Quebec where he died on the Plains of Abraham, in the moment of victory over Montcalm who himself fell mortally wounded in the moment of defeat. Later, Washington would hear how the French surrendered Venango, Presque Isle, Niagara, Detroit, Mackinac, and Vincennes.

With the Forks of the Ohio in their possession, a fecund people could move into the West by flatboat, keelboat, horseback, and covered wagon. They would tarry at one frontier for a generation, then new generations would push the frontier on and ever on. They could always see brighter rainbows in the West, for they were of a breed born with rainbows in their eyes.

Although Washington's approaching marriage and his landholdings in Virginia would tie him to the East, he would remain a westerner at heart. A year before Daniel Boone moved his family to Kentucky, Washington already had sailed by boat down the Ohio as far as the Great Kanawha to claim lands and millsites granted for his services in the war. On that voyage he rode gunwale to gunwale at the forefront of the tide of English-speaking men and women sweeping west, to inundate the French populations in the forest clearings, cross the Mississippi, well up the ramp of the sunbright plains, lap across the Shining Mountains and down the western slope to where the sun each day is quenched in what was once the Spanish Sea.

As these people moved West they would come to places with such exotic names as Baton Rouge, Cache la Poudre, Des Moines, Duluth, Pierre, Laramie, Boise, and Coeur d'Alene. There they would rear large families of English-speaking children, who would grow up in those places without a thought of the brave but vanquished people who put those enchanting names in our geography.

These people with rainbows in their eyes came to creeks and mountains and valleys for which the French had left no remembered names. They, therefore, bestowed names of their own, and the name they bestowed most often was Washington.

All over our land, schools, streets, and squares bear the name of Washington, as do the capital of the United States, a state of the Union, 31 counties, and 43 post offices. For good measure 20 more post offices are called Mount Vernon.

Time has not dimmed the memory of Washington. This is evidenced by a million and more people, who every year journey to America's most loved historic shrine, Mount Vernon, drawn there for no reason other than that George and Martha Washington once lived there.

As directed by General Forbes, Colonel Washington took the Forbes Road for home to ask Governor Fauquier for winter garb for his troops. At Loyalhanna his horse fagged out. But another man with a fresher mount, bound for Virginia, carried Washington's urgent letter to Fauquier, begging for garments for his men. As soon as he could proceed, Washington rode as far as Winchester, where he fell ill and again was delayed. Once more he wrote the governor, pleading for his shivering Virginians. Finally he made it to Williamsburg to present his request in person. Fauquier assured him that there were not enough made up coats in Virginia, but there were woolen blankets. These had been tailored into coats and were on the way.

Duty performed, Washington crossed the Pamunkey at the ferry and arrived at the White House, where on January 6, 1759, he and Martha were married by 69-year-old David Mosson, the Anglican rector of the parish. For a honeymoon tour they visited Williamsburg, where, on call of the governor, the Burgesses assembled on February 22, Washington's twenty-seventh birthday.

There Washington was sworn in as one of the two members from Winchester and took the hard, straight-backed seat assigned to him. There occurred an incident of which no verbatum record has been preserved. We must depend, therefore, on the memory of Edmund Randolph, who was only six years old at the time and who probably was not there, but who could have obtained the details from his father, John Randolph, clerk of the House, or from his uncle, Peyton Randolph, a Burgess. At any rate he is credited with the story, which was not published until after Washington's death.

Randolph's story has it that after the House had completed the preliminaries of organization, a member moved that the Burgesses express the thanks of Virginia to the colonel. It was carried with enthusiasm. Speaker Robinson put the thanks in the form of words. And who was better fitted than Robinson, a natural orator, who had been Washington's friend and supporter since that winter day when he came back from carrying the message to Le Boeuf? Robinson, stylishly bewigged, genteelly rotund, perfectly self-assured, spoke words that glowed.

When he had done, the man who at Jumonville Glen had thought the whistle of bullets as somewhat charming, felt all eyes on him. There were the two Randolphs, two Lees, four Carters, a Bland, a Mason, a Pendleton, a Wythe, and other distinguished personages from the first families of Virginia. Their eyes looked as though they expected him to respond.

He rose to his feet. He blushed so red it showed through the tan of his cheeks. He shook from the silver buckles of his shoes to the crown of his scalp. He was good to look at, straight as a forest pine, slender as on the day he offered his services to Dinwiddie. His lips moved, but they stammered not an intelligible syllable. Thereupon, Robinson showed his friendship most effectively by exclaiming: "Sit down, Mr. Washington. Your modesty is equal to your valor, and that surpasses the power of any language that I possess."

Index

origin of the name, 10
line of ownership, 85 f
shrine to Washington, 225
Muse, George
under Colonel Fry, 72
made lieutenant colonel, 73
cowardly at Fort Necessity, 78
rebuked, 82

Niagara
campaign against, 129 ff

Old Briton
Miami chief, 26, 32 f
death battle, 35
Ohio Company, 17, 25, 28

Pacifists
Society of Friends, 138
Indians, 199
Post, Christian F., 200
Penn, William
wins Indians, 43 f
Pennington, Isaac
shelters Washington, 13
Pennsylvanians
demand military law, 142
Pickawillany
Miami village, 16, 26, 32, 33, 35
Pitt, William
heads government, 163
Pittsburgh, founding of, 221
Post, Christian F., 201, 202, 206
pacifist, 200
promotes Indian neutrality, 200
gets peace agreement signed, 221
Primogeniture, 9
Profanity
Washington's action against, 159

Raystown Path, 178
Roads
building process, 64 ff, 212
Robinson, John
Virginia burgess, 56, 123
tribute to Washington, 227
Rogers, Robert
fame of, 149 ff
Rogers' Rangers, 149 ff, 155, 163 f

St. Clair, Sir John
under Braddock, 98

commissary under Forbes, 169,
173, 177
St. Pierre, Legardeur de
at Fort Le Boeuf, 37, 48
killed, 118
Scurvey
at Fort Ontario, 130 f
Seven Years' War, 132
Sharpe, Horatio
commander in Southern colonies, 84 f
builds Fort Cumberland, 85
belittles colonial officers, 85
favors Dagworthy, 126, 128
Shirley, William
to take Fort Niagara, 87
builds Fort Ontario, 118
colonial chief, 126
sides with Washington, 128
plans attack on Niagara, 129
retired, proved no traitor, 133
Shirley, William, Jr., 90
killed, 109
Smallpox, kills Indians, 156
Smith, James, 96, 103 f, 115 f, 119
Stobo, Robert
Scotsman, joins Washington, 73
helps finish Fort Necessity, 76
hostage, 81, 84
makes map of Fort Duquesne, 98
named a spy, 117
Stanwix, John
commander of Southern forces,
153
made brigadier general, 168

Trent, William, 55
frontiersman, 2, 16, 41
fails as Dinwiddie's messenger, 2 f
builds Fort George, 55
recruiting, 59
negotiates with Indians, 60

Uniform, 171, 196

Van Braam, Jacob
teaches Washington swordsmanship, 38
interpreter, 39, 48 f, 68, 71
faulty translator, 80 f, 82